ASIAPAC CULTURE

Origins of
CHINESE
PEOPLE and CUSTOMS

Compiled by Li Xiaoxiang   Illustrated by Fu Chunjiang
Translated by Geraldine Goh

⚚ ASIAPAC • SINGAPORE

Publisher
ASIAPAC BOOKS PTE LTD
996 Bendemeer Road #06-09
Singapore 339944
Tel: (65) 6392 8455
Fax: (65) 6392 6455
Email: asiapacbooks@pacific.net.sg

Come visit us at our Internet home page
www.asiapacbooks.com

First published December 2001
9th edition February 2008

© 2001 ASIAPAC BOOKS, SINGAPORE
ISBN 13 978-981-229-384-8
ISBN10   981-229-384-1

Cover illustrations by Fu Chunjiang
Cover design by Chin Boon Leng and Kelly Lim
Body text in 11pt Times New Roman
Printed in Singapore by Loi Printing

Publisher's Note

Why are Chinese customs still practised worldwide? Surely it is because they still bear great significance and meaning today.

Be it the practice of obstructing a groom with a barricade of maidens demanding a big, fat red packet; the many do's and don'ts that a new mother has to observe; or the act of protecting one's child with glittering bracelets or tinkling anklets — they all perform important or meaningful functions. They are a crystallisation of the wisdom of the Chinese people and have withstood the test of time.

Origins of Chinese People and Customs unveils the naming system, birth customs, death rituals, wedding ceremonies and social etiquette of the Chinese. It also introduces readers to the origins of the Chinese people, and provides the answers to questions like: "Why are the Chinese known as 'descendants of Yanhuang' or 'descendants of the dragon'?"

Each chapter includes a legend that is related to the topic. Be enthralled by the many delightful accounts — like the legends of Huang Di and Yan Di, the origins of the practice of teasing newlyweds in the bridal chamber, and the reason behind burning joss paper for the deceased.

We would like to take this opportunity to thank Fu Chunjiang for his illustrations, Li Xiaoxiang for her compilation, and Geraldine Goh for her translation. Our appreciation, too, to the production team for their best efforts in putting this book together.

ORIGINS OF CHINESE MUSIC

Covers everything a music enthusiast wants to know about Chinese music: origins and history; Chinese musical instruments; classical masterpieces; and musicians of ancient China.
ISBN 978-981-229-475-3

Preface to the Chinese Culture Series

Tens of thousands of years ago, the eastern part of the northern hemisphere was a wide expanse of land which was populated by a group of people. They learnt to gather wood and make fires. They started to hunt, fish and farm. They invented written text. They created culture. They established a nation.

They were the earliest Huaxia people who prospered and multiplied to become the largest ethnic group on Earth. They developed by leaps and bounds to forge a dazzling culture. Many a brilliant ancient civilisation has been swallowed up by the currents of time, but the Huaxia culture has managed to survive. In fact, it continues to exert its influence today, not only within China, but also without, via the Silk Road, migration, etc.

The flames of wars erupted. Dynasties rose and fell. Despite the changing faces of political power, the essence of the Chinese people has remained unchanged.

Today, the Chinese people are not merely an ethnic group, but a larger cultural entity spread all over the world.

The most distinguishing aspect of Chinese culture is its all-encompassing nature. It emphasises justice and moral integrity, human relations, the power of music and rituals to cultivate the hearts of men, and the oneness of Man and Heaven... all at the same time. Next is its wisdom — it engineers invention and change, and is prolific and dynamic. Last but not least is its ingenuity — it is ever progressive and enlightening.

Taking a flying leap into the global lake of the world, the ancient Chinese culture exudes the vitality of youth!

Li Xiaoxiang ·
11 November 2001

About the Compiler

Li Xiaoxiang 李小香 was born in 1946. After graduating from Hu'nan Normal University in 1969, she taught Chinese language and literature in a high school. Later, she worked in Zhejiang University as a staff member of the Higher Education Research Department, an Office Administrator in the Economics Department, and as editor of an academic journal.

Besides having a firm foundation in Chinese language and literature, Li is also skilled in editorial work. She has a deep understanding of traditional Chinese culture, especially Buddhism, and has penned several discourses on this subject.

With her penchant for writing, she has produced 20-odd literary pieces and works on various topics. Her published works for the children's market include *The Story of Xinqiji, The Story of a Junior Barber, The Story of a Fisherman and a Goldfish*, and *Wisdom in Chinese Proverbs*.

She is presently a Senior Editor with Wuhan University Press.

About the Illustrator

Fu Chunjiang, born in 1974, is a native of Chongqing municipality in southeastern China. A lover of traditional Chinese culture, he graduated in Chinese language studies.

He has been fond of drawing from childhood, and since 1994, he has been drawing comics. Among his works are *The Story of Kites* and *The Faint-Hearted Hero,* as well as the bestsellers *Origins of Chinese Festivals* and *Origins of Chinese People & Customs* published by Asiapac Books. He also participated in the production of *One Riddle for One Story.*

Contents

PROLOGUE

On the vast land of China live 56 diverse ethnic groups. Together, they have created the impressive Chinese civilisation.

Ancient script of *hua* 华

From Flower to Chinese

The Chinese people are also known as *huaren* 华人. The original meaning of the character *hua* 华 is flower. Look at the ancient script. Doesn't it look like a flower in full blossom? A world without flowers would be so much the duller. Later, the meaning of *hua* broadened to refer to beauty, goodness and brilliance.

3

Map of China

China has a vast expanse of land. It is, in fact, the fourth largest country in the world. Some people say that the outline of the map of China is shaped like a rooster. Do you agree?

ORIGINS OF THE CHINESE PEOPLE

The Earliest Ancestors

The ancient name of China is "Huaxia 华夏", meaning a prosperous and beautiful land in the central plains.

Huaxia is a combination of the names of two ancient Chinese tribes — the Huaxu tribe 华胥氏 and the Xia tribe 夏族. The Huaxu tribe is much more ancient than the Xia tribe. They were the earliest ancestors of the Chinese people.

Fuxi Invents the Eight Trigrams

Fuxi 伏羲 is said to have a human head and the body of a snake. Nüwa 女娲, the goddess who created Man with a lump of clay, was his sister and wife. Fuxi created the famous Eight Trigrams and transmitted the knowledge to the human race. He said that by mastering the principles of these symbols, Man would gain the wisdom of the gods.

Nüwa holds the moon in her hand. On the moon, there is a mythical toad. It's a symbol of Nüwa as the Moon Goddess.

Fuxi holds the sun in his hand. On the sun there is a golden crow. It's a symbol of Fuxi as the Sun God.

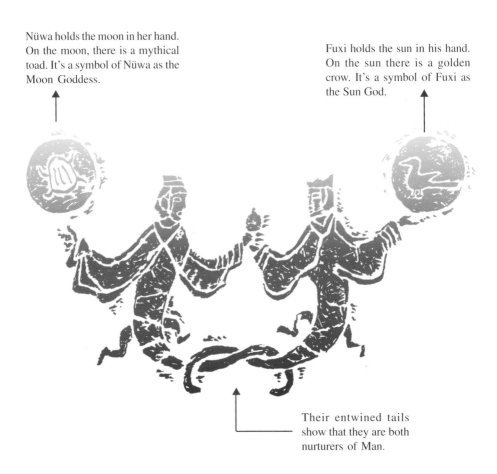

Their entwined tails show that they are both nurturers of Man.

Fuxi and Nüwa

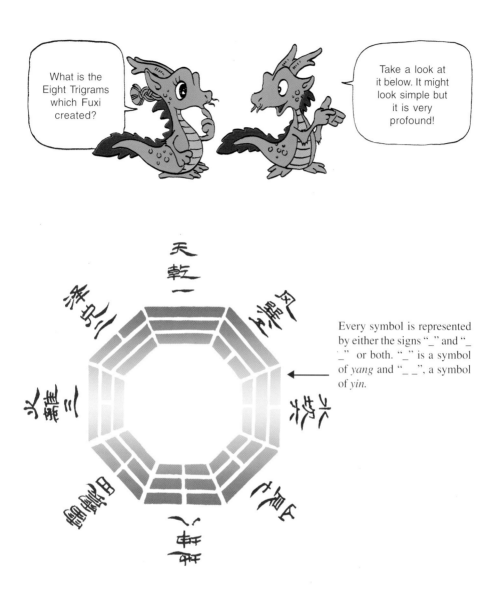

What is the Eight Trigrams which Fuxi created?

Take a look at it below. It might look simple but it is very profound!

Every symbol is represented by either the signs "_" and "_ _" or both. "_" is a symbol of *yang* and "_ _", a symbol of *yin*.

The Eight Trigrams is made up of eight symbols. The symbols are *qian* 乾, *kun* 坤, *zhen* 震, *xun* 巽, *kan* 坎, *li* 离, *gen* 艮 and *dui* 兑. These symbols look simple, but in them lie profound laws and principles. To put it simply, the Eight Trigrams purports that the universe is not a creation of the gods, but a make-up of eight elements of the natural world. These eight elements are Heaven, Earth, Thunder, Wind, Water, Fire, Mountain and Marsh.

Descendants of Yanhuang

The Chinese people often call themselves the descendants of Yanhuang. Yanhuang refers to the progeny of Fuxi — Huang Di 黄帝 (the Yellow Emperor) and Yan Di 炎帝 (the Fire Emperor). Let us look at Huang Di first.

Huang Di
He had four faces facing the north, south, east and west respectively. He dominated the regions of the Yellow River and put a stop to the protracted fighting among the various tribes. He created the embryonic system of a country, propelling the Chinese people into an age of civilisation.

Huang Di also created the ceremonial costume of the ruler, wearing a yellow robe and a yellow headdress. Yellow, symbolising the colour of the earth, became the colour specifically used by only kings and emperors.

Huang Di taught his people to domesticate animals.

He also taught them to build houses, freeing them from primitive cave-dwelling life.

Huang Di was also a brilliant physician. Later generations compiled his knowledge of the art of healing into the earliest medical compendium, *The Yellow Emperor's Medicine Classic* 《黄帝内经》.

Huang Di's wife Leizu reared silkworm to produce silk which was used to make clothes. Thereafter, Man no longer wore animal skin and leaves.

Cangjie, one of Huang Di's officials, invented writing. The invention gave Man a means of communicating with each other.

Huang Di cast *ding* 鼎 (a kind of vessel with two loop handles) and *zhong* 钟 (cups without handles), laid down the rules of etiquette and invented the calendar.

Yan Di

He is also known as Shen Nong 神农 (Holy Farmer). As the father of Chinese agriculture, he had made great contributions to Chinese civilisation.

Yan Di taught Man to grow the five grains and to farm.

Yan Di tasted hundreds of herbs, identifying varieties which could be used as medicine. As a result, Man's knowledge of herbal medicine increased.

Yan Di the Holy Farmer

Yan Di invented the axe, the hoe and many other farming tools.

Yan Di invented the *qin* 琴 (the zither), *se* 瑟 (stringed instrument similar to the zither) and other musical instruments. He made great contributions to Chinese music.

Yan Di made earthenware to hold water, keep food and store grains.

Chinese Primitive Man

Oh! So frightening! Whose bones are these?

These bones are very valuable.

Archeologists painstakingly unearthed them. They are the bones of the earliest Chinese people.

Yuanmou Man

An archeologist discovered the fossil teeth of a Chinese primitive man in the County of Yuanmou in Yunnan Province. The bones date back to 1.7 million years ago. This is the oldest fossil rock discovered of the Chinese primitive man.

Lantian Man

The fossil of the Lantian Man was discovered in the county of Lantian in Shaanxi County. It is 700,000 years old.

Peking Man

The fossil of the Peking Man was discovered in Zhoukoudian in the outskirts of Beijing. His skull is about 500,000 years old.

The primitive man was a hunter-gatherer. He lived in natural caves and shaped hunting weapons out of rocks.

Culture of the New Stone Age

In 1921, archaeologists found New Stone Age ruins that date from some 5,000 to 7,000 years ago in Mianchi, He'nan Province. They named it "Yangshao" culture.

On this site, they discovered colourful pottery decorated with red and black motifs. This shows that people back then already knew how to use fire to mould earth for the creation of vessels like basins, bowls, cups, plates and jars to store cooked food and raw grains. In contrast, Old Stone Age people used the skins of fruit or bones of animals as vessels.

These earthern vessels are beautiful works of art. Back then, the people already had an eye for aesthetics and art.

The main production tools used included stone axes, stone knives, fish hooks and fish forks. They had also invented powerful hunting weapons like bows and arrows. They domesticated and reared pigs, dogs, goats, chickens, horses and oxen. They also grew chestnuts, Chinese cabbages and leaf mustard. They no longer dwelled in caves and were able to construct simple huts. Though basic, these huts were safer and more comfortable than caves. The people were able to sleep soundly without fear of snakes and wild beasts.

The Chinese people

The Huaxia people and other tribes intermingled over time to become one race — the Han Chinese. In the past, the Huaxia people believed the Central Plains was the centre of the world. They called the land where they lived Zhonghua 中华 (*zhong* meaning centre) or Zhongguo 中国 (Middle Kingdom).

Besides the Han Chinese, there are minority nationalities like the Tibetans, the Mongolians, the Bais, the Kazakh people and the Uighurs. Together, they are known as the Chinese people.

Han
nationality

Tibetan
nationality

**The Chinese
People**

Bai
nationality

Mongol
nationality

Uighur nationality

Kazakh nationality

Fuxi Teaches His People to Fish With a Net

In primitive times, people did not know how to farm. Hunting and fishing were the main means of livelihood.

It's not easy to catch fish. If there's a way to make the task easier, everyone can have fish as often as he wishes and won't go hungry again.

The spider spins a web to catch its prey...

Aha, I've got it!

Ha, ha! This is great! No one has to worry about going without fish.

Then, he taught his people to weave nets and to use them to catch fish. Since then, people have been using fishing nets to catch fish.

With a vine he found in the mountain, Fuxi wove a net.

Huang Di's Battle Against Chiyou

When Huang Di was in power, Chiyou, a fearless and barbaric tribal chief, often harassed the other tribes.

Huang Di led his army and clashed with Chiyou at Zhuolu. Chiyou brought forth a huge blanket of fog.

Oh no, we're lost!

Huang Di's subordinate Fenghou built a compass carriage and led the army out of the heavy fog.

But the cunning Chiyou got the Wind God and the Rain God to stir up a storm. Huang Di and his men were trapped in the stormy sea.

Seeing this, Huang Di's daughter Ba* hurried to the battlefield. Immediately, the wind and rain subsided and the sun began to shine.

Father, I've come to help you.

* Ba is a spirit that brings drought.

15

A woman suddenly appeared before Huang Di just as he was thinking hard about how he should deal with the enemy.

I'm Goddess Xuannü. I am here to offer you a strategy.

Following Goddess Xuannü's instructions, Huang Di used the skin of a monster to make a huge battle drum.

Then, at Thunder Marsh, he slayed the Thunder Monster and took its biggest bone to make drumsticks.

On the battlefield...

Beat the drum!

Huang Di succeeded in killing Chiyou, and the tribes were able to live in peace and harmony again.

Boom!
Boom!

Chiyou's men were terrified. The whole army collapsed.

Shen Nong Tastes Hundreds of Plants

In ancient times, crops, herbs, plants and flowers grew side by side in one big mess. It was hard to tell them apart.

People hunt for a living. But when animals and birds dwindle in numbers, they have to endure hunger. When they fall ill, there is no medicine to treat them.

I must find some way to prevent them from going hungry and to cure them when they fall sick.

I will taste all the plants here to find out which can satisfy hunger and which can treat illnesses.

One day, Shen Nong tasted a poisonous plant.

King, it's too dangerous for you to taste herbs like this.

The people are waiting for me to find out which plants are edible and which have medicinal properties.

Later, Shen Nong used tea leaves to neutralise the poison, and carried on tasting the plants. Finally, Shen Nong discovered the five grains (rice, two kinds of millet, wheat and beans) and 365 kinds of medicinal herbs.

With this knowledge, the people cultivated the five grains and grew medicinal herbs. They no longer had to starve or leave their illnesses untreated.

17

THE DRAGON'S DESCENDANTS

The dragon is truly a great symbol of the Chinese people. The Chinese often proudly refer to themselves as the descendants of the dragon!

Totemism

The Chinese dragon has a history of over 6,000 years. Research shows that the dragon was probably created by combining the features of different totems, the chief form being the snake.

In ancient times, people often used beasts and even plants which they feared as a sign of their tribe. By worshipping the sign, they hoped to be protected from harm. This is totemism.

China was a tribal society in those days. Each tribe worshipped its own totem.

Tiger totem

Ox totem

Snake totem

Bird totem

People began to worship the dragon. They fused forces of nature like thunder, lightning and rain with this creature.

Boom!

Look, everybody!

The dragon has transformed into lightning and flown up into the sky!

Oh! What a loud roar! It's really frightening.

Hurray! The dragon has brought us rain.

In time, the dragon was even endowed with the powers of god. Even though the days of worshipping totems were over, the dragon still occupies an important position in the hearts of the people.

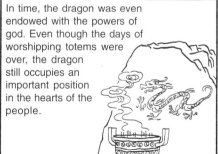

The Dragon

In ancient times, the Chinese viewed the dragon as an extremely powerful, noble and mysterious beast. It could swim in the sea and summon the wind and the rain. This divine mythical creature was believed to bring with it abundance, prosperity, good fortune and divine protection. It is a symbol of power, excellence, boldness, heroism, nobility and divinity.

Unlike their Western counterparts which were associated with negative characteristics, most Eastern dragons were seen as peaceable and sagacious creatures. Instead of being feared, they were loved and worshipped. That is why many Chinese cities have pagodas where people could burn incense and pray to dragons. Since they were unable to control it the way they controlled other beasts, they prayed to it for protection, good weather and bumper harvests.

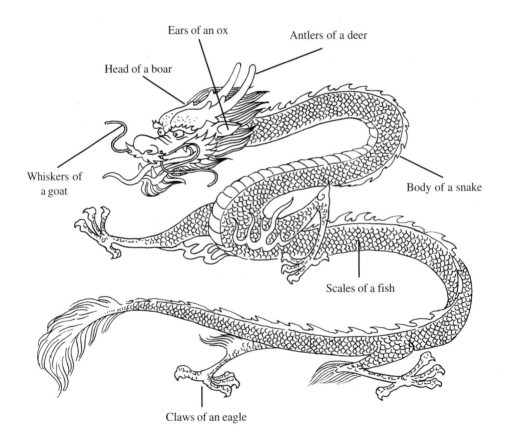

Ears of an ox

Antlers of a deer

Head of a boar

Whiskers of a goat

Body of a snake

Scales of a fish

Claws of an eagle

Symbols of the dragon

The dragon was also a symbol of imperial power. The emperor's body was called the dragon's body and his face, the dragon's face. He wore the dragon robe, sat on the dragon chair and slept on the dragon bed. His descendants were called the dragon's descendants.

Dragon dance

Dragon temples were built to worship the dragon. On festive days, people would twirl the dragon lantern and perform the dragon dance. The dragon thus became a symbol of celebration.

Dragon festivals

There are all kinds of dragon festivals. For example, on festive occasions like the Dragon Worship Festival and the Spring Dragon Festival, people pray for favourable weather and bumper harvests, and consume dragon beard noodles and dragon scale biscuits. During the Dragon Boat Festival, dragon boat races are held.

Types of Chinese Dragons

The first Chinese dragon
Found in an old grave dating back to the time of Yangshao Culture 6,000 years ago, this is the earliest dragon discovered. The motif of a dragon is depicted with clam shells.

Jade dragon
Unearthed in Inner Mongolia, this dragon has a history of about 5,000 years.

Five-clawed giant dragon
During the Yuan, Ming and Qing Dynasties, the emperor's robe and the decorations in the palace depicted the five-clawed giant dragon. Commoners who used the five-clawed giant dragon as an ornament would be beheaded.

Elephant dragon
This dragon is popular in regions where lamaism is widespread, like Mongolia and Manchuria.

Ying dragon

It has two wings and a tail which resembles that of a fish or a seahorse. It either has one horn or two teeth-like horns.

Green dragon

This is one of the four mythical animals of China. The other three are the red phoenix, the white tiger and the tortoise.

The Development of the Character "Dragon"

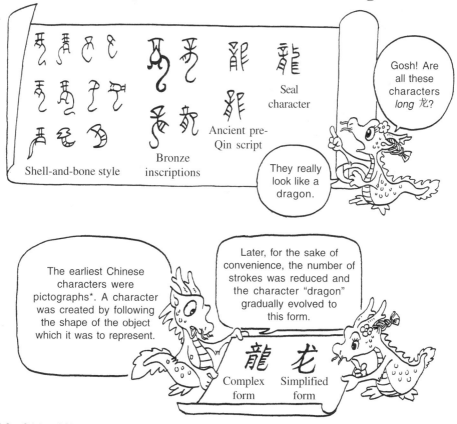

Seal character

Ancient pre-Qin script

Bronze inscriptions

Shell-and-bone style

Gosh! Are all these characters *long* 龙?

They really look like a dragon.

The earliest Chinese characters were pictographs*. A character was created by following the shape of the object which it was to represent.

Later, for the sake of convenience, the number of strokes was reduced and the character "dragon" gradually evolved to this form.

龍　尤

Complex form　Simplified form

* See Origins of Chinese Music and Art *for more information on Chinese writing.*

The Carp Leaps Over the Dragon Gate

Legend has it that in an attempt to control the floodwaters, Yu* split apart the mountain that blocked the flow of the Yellow River. The waters of the Yellow River came crashing down. Later generations named these falls "Yu's Gate".

* For the full story on Yu's great feat, please turn to page 30.

If it's blocked, there will be flooding again and the people will suffer.

Can you jump over the opening?

It's much too high!

It's too tough.

Well then, I'll propose to the Jade Emperor to transform those who succeed in leaping over into a flying dragon.

It's worth a try.

All right.

From then on, come late spring, shoals of carp would swim against the current of the Yellow River, gather at Yu's Gate and try their utmost to scale the falls.

Those who succeed in jumping over are at once transformed into a dragon that could fly high up into the sky.

How I envy him!

Yu's Gate was later known as the Dragon Gate. That is how the ancient Chinese saying "Once the carp leaps over Dragon Gate, its value increases tenfold" came about. Successful candidates of the Imperial Examination were said to have scaled the Dragon Gate.

THE YELLOW RIVER

A dragon-like river

The long history of Chinese civilisation began from a river. The river, measuring 5,464 km long, is like a long and winding gigantic dragon. It is known as the Yellow River because of its yellow water.

A nurturing river

The volume of soil carried by the Yellow River is the largest in the world. The deposited silt form huge plains whose soft texture and richness make them ideal for the cultivation of crops.

The cradle of Chinese civilisation

Somewhere around 5,000 BC, tribal Chinese ancestors settled down at the river basin of the Yellow River. They cultivated millet and grains from generation to generation in the rich alluvial soil washed down by the river. It marked the beginnings of the long history of the Chinese people.

Battling the Yellow River

The Yellow River is the foundation of Chinese civilisation, but its torrential waters often break the banks, causing serious floods. Controlling the river waters is a very difficult task. Since the days of yore, the Chinese people have continuously attempted to subdue this tempestuous river with their courage, determination and wits.

Great Yu Controls the Floodwaters

The Yellow River often broke its banks, causing serious flooding. People built dams and dykes to prevent the river water from overflowing. Still, that did not stop the floodwaters. Agricultural land and homes were inundated.

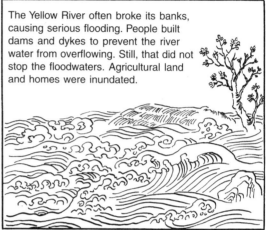

The dykes fail to stop the floodwaters.

I must find a better solution.

In ancient times, there was a hero who succeeded in controlling the floodwaters. He was Yu. His father Kun had been put to death for failing in this endeavour.

Yu made drastic changes to his father's method of building dykes. He had channels constructed to lead the waters into the sea.

Though Yu passed by his home three times while working on his flood-control project, each time, he did not stop.

When the water is controlled, I will return home.

King Shun

Yu, you've made a great contribution by controlling the floodwaters. I'll abdicate in your favour.

Thirteen years later, Yu finally completed his flood-control project.

CHINESE NAMES AND SURNAMES

The Chinese have a complicated system of forms of address. To them, the name is not merely a form of address but also of great significance.

CHINESE SURNAMES

Let's look at the character *xing* 姓 (surname):

$$\text{片} + \text{坐} = \text{片坐}$$

It is made up of two parts: *nü* 女 (woman) and *sheng* 生 (birth) indicating that it is a woman who gives birth. This is an implication that in primitive times, China was a matriarchal society. Children knew who their mother was but not their father.

Matriarchal society

The mother was the central figure of the family. Children born of the same mother formed a group called the maternal tribe.

To avoid intermarriages within the tribe, the surname became the title of the clan. In the matriarchal society, children took their mother's surname. Those with the same surname were not allowed to marry.

Ancient surnames

Many ancient surnames carry the radical *nü* 女 . The surnames of the ancestors of the Huaxia people and some benevolent kings in ancient times also had this radical.

Creation of Surnames

Statistics show that there are more than 8,000 Chinese surnames. But there are only 200 to 300 common ones. How did these surnames come about? There are a few ways to create surnames:

Using the totem
Totems like the dragon, horse, pig, mountain, cloud and wind were worshipped by different tribes.

The totem of my tribe is the horse. My surname is Ma 马 (horse).

Using the name of one's state
Examples include Qi 齐, Lu 鲁, Song 宋 and Wei 卫. These are names of states.

I'm a native of the State of Qi. My surname is Qi.

The king bestowed a fiefdom on my ancestors in the city of Zhao 赵. I'll take Zhao as my surname.

Using the name of one's fief
For example, in Western Zhou, there was a man by the name of Zaofu. He was rewarded with a fiefdom by Duke Mu of Zhou in the Zhao City. Zaofu's descendants took on the surname of Zhao.

Using the title of an official post

For example, Sima 司马 (Minister of War), Situ 司徒 (Minister of Land and People) and Sikong 司空 (Minister of Public Works) were titles of official posts in ancient times.

I'm the Minister of War (Sima 司马). All my descendants shall take the name of my position as their surname.

I'm a potter. My surname is Tao 陶 (pottery) of course.

Using the name of one's occupation

For example, the ancestors of those whose surname is Tao were probably potters. Shamans and witchdoctors probably took on the surname Wu 巫.

Using the landmark of the place where one resided

Ximen 西门 (west gate), Liu 柳 (willow) and Chi 池 (pond) are just some examples. It is likely that these people lived near the west gate, some willow trees or a pond.

My surname is Liu 柳.

Most Chinese surnames consist of a single character. Common surnames are Zhang 张, Wang 王, Li 李 Zhao 赵, Liu 刘, Chen 陈, Lin 林, Yang 杨, Xu 徐, Zhou 周 and Huang 黄. There are also surnames with two characters, like Sima 司马, Shangguan 上官 and Ouyang 欧阳. Generally, the Chinese do not marry someone with the same surname.

Now let's look at the origins of some common Chinese surnames.

Origins of the Surname Li 李

The origins of Li can be traced to the late Shang Dynasty and early Zhou Dynasty. Its original form was 理(Li) and was first used by Gaoyao. He served King Yao as a senior justice officer. The position was named Dali 大理. Later, Gaoyao's descendants inherited his post.

By the Shang Dynasty, it was the norm for the names of official positions to be used as the surname. Thus, Gaoyao's descendants took on the surname Li 理.

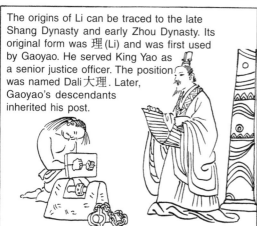

King Zhou of the late Shang Dynasty was a despotic tyrant. One of Gaoyao's descendants, Li Zheng 理徵, boldly pointed out his mistakes, and urged him to mend his ways. King Zhou was furious and killed him. Li Zheng's wife fled with her young son Li Lizhen 理利真 to the west of He'nan.

Mother and son arrived at the ruins of the Yi tribe settlement at the river basin of the Yi River. They were hungry, thirsty and totally exhausted.

Mother, can we eat this wild fruit?

Sure, *muzi* can quench your thirst and sate your hunger.

They lived on *muzi* and survived. Grateful for the wild fruit, and also to avoid King Zhou's persecution, Li Lizhen combined the two characters of *muzi* 木子 to create the character *li* 李. He used that as his surname, thus changing his name to 李利真 (Li Lizhen). This is how the surname Li came about.

Famous personalities with the surname Li:

Li Bai is the name of the famous Tang poet.

Li Er is the name of Laozi, the great philosopher who lived during the Spring and Autumn period.

Li was the surname of the emperors of the Tang Dynasty.

Origins of the Surname Zhao 赵

Zaofu was a carriage driver serving Duke Mu of Zhou.

One day, Duke Mu headed west and went hunting in a carriage drawn by swift steeds. Upon arriving at Mt Kunlun, he drank and sang with the Queen Mother of the West and forgot to return.

At this time, Duke Xuyan in the southeast rebelled. Zaofu's driving skills were fully displayed as he travelled thousands of *li* in just a day. They returned in time.

Duke Mu launched an attack and defeated Duke Xuyan.

Zaofu, you've helped to suppress the rebellion. I bestow on you the city of Zhao 赵.

Thank you, Sire!

The descendants of Zaofu used the name of the city of Zhao as their surname. Zaofu became the ancestor of the Zhaos.

Famous personalities with the surname Zhao:

Zhao was the surname of Song emperors.

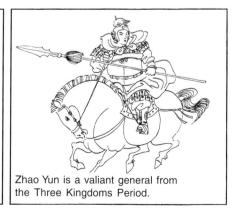

Zhao Yun is a valiant general from the Three Kingdoms Period.

Origins of the Surname Liu 刘

It is said that King Yao's surname is Yinqi 尹祁. A branch of his descendants adopted Qi 祁 as their surname. They were given land in Liuguo 刘国.

Liu Lei, a descendant of the Qi branch, acquired the knowledge of rearing dragons from Huanlong.

Famous personalities with the surname Liu:

Liu was the surname of Han emperors.

Liu Bowen is a famous military tactician from the Ming Dynasty.

Liu Lei failed to keep the dragons alive and fled with his family to the Lu County. He remained in hiding there. All his descendants bore the surname Liu 刘.

Origins of the Surname Chen 陈

After King Wu of Zhou toppled the Shang Dynasty, he conferred titles and land on the descendants of good officials. On finding King Shun's descendant Gui Man, King Wu married his eldest daughter, Yuanji, to him and gave him the title "Marquis Chen".

Yao married his two daughters to Shun and let them settle down by River Guirui. Their descendants who remained by River Guirui took on the surname Gui 妫.

His descendants took on the surname Chen 陈.

Famous personalities with the surname Chen:

Tang poet Chen Zi'ang

Chinese patriot in modern times, Chen Jiageng (Tan Kah Kee)

Origins of the Surname Lin 林

King Zhou, the last king of the Shang Dynasty, was a tyrannical sadist who took pleasure in torturing and killing the innocent.

Loyal official Bigan remonstrated with the king and was put to death.

Bigan's wife, who was pregnant, escaped to the forest and later gave birth to a son.

After King Wu of Zhou destroyed the Shang regime, he bestowed the name Lin 林 on Bigan's son, and also made him his official.

Famous personalities with the surname Lin:

Modern writer Lin Yutang

Lin Zexu, the Qing official who stamped out opium

Origins of the Surname Zhang 张

Hao's son Hui was said to have invented the bow.

The bow and arrow are the most important weapons. I'll make you Supervisor of the Bow and Arrow Makers.

Your surname shall be Zhang 张.

The old script of Zhang resembles that of a man drawing his bow. That is how the surname Zhang came about.

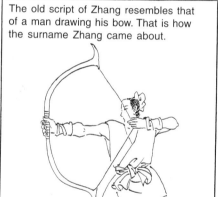

Famous personalities with the surname Zhang:

Zhang Qian, the diplomat who opened the Silk Road

Zhang Heng, a scientist during the Eastern Zhou Dynasty

43

CHINESE NAMES

There is a rich variety of Chinese names. You can give any name you wish. However, parents usually give names that connote good luck or the realisation of beautiful dreams.

Often, every name has a special meaning. For example, Fu 福 (fortune), Fu 富 (wealth), Cai 财 (riches) and Gui 贵 (prestige) are names that show a desire to gain wealth and prosperity. Kang 康 (good health), Shou 寿 (longevity), Jian 健 (good health and strength) and Song 松 (pine) all indicate the wish for a long and healthy life.

Words that denote strength and power are often used in names for boys to reflect their masculinity.

Girls are usually given gentler names to connote beauty and softness.

Names with two characters outnumber those with a single character.

Li Meimei	Xu Ziqiang	Zhang Ling	Wu Feng
(two characters)	(two characters)	(one character)	(one character)

Common Character

In some families, a common character is used in each sibling's name. For example:

It is also possible to use a common character for names within the clan. These common clan characters were long decided by the ancestors of the family. The common characters for 12 generations or more can be stated at one go. With common clan characters, every member of the clan is given a name which corresponds to his rank (in terms of generation) in the clan.

Common characters of the Kong family

During the Qing Dynasty, Emperor Qian Long set down 30 common characters for Confucius and his descendants. A descendant, Kong Lingyi, later added another 20 more. These 50 common characters are listed in order from left to right as follows:

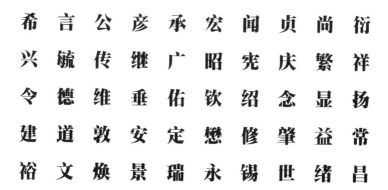

During the Song and Yuan Dynasties, commoners without a trade or occupation were not allowed to have names. How did they call their babies then?

Interesting Ancient Naming Methods

Since he's our third child, let's call him Xiaosanzi 小三子 (Little third son).

Call him Wujiu 五九 (Five nine). I'm 22 and you're 23. The sum of 22 and 23 is 45. And 5 x 9 gives 45.

Hmm, doesn't he weigh seven *jin*? Let's call him Qijin 七斤 (Seven *jin*).

During the Spring and Autumn Period and Warring States Period, it was fashionable to give one's children demeaning or repulsive names. Some children were named after diseases while some boys were given girls' names.

Demeaning and repulsive names
Duke Jinhui named his daughter Qie 妾 (concubine) while Duke Luwen named his son E 恶 (evil).

Disease-inspired names
Gongshucuo (where *cuo* 痤 means acne)

Female names for men
Xigu, Xufuren, where *gu* 姑 and *furen* 夫人 are terms that apply only to women

Names with auxiliary words
Zhuzhiwu, Hanbuxin, where *zhi* 之 and *bu* 不 are auxiliary words

Ways of Calling Chinese Names

Take note, however, that a married Chinese woman might take her husband's surname, or she might put her husband's surname before her maiden surname. For example, you may address Wang-Li Huiyun as Mrs Wang or Madam Li.

NAMES AND FORTUNE

All sorts of methods have been created to pick a good and auspicious name. If a person's life has not been going well, it is possible to change his luck by changing his name. These methods have no scientific basis, but they reflect everyone's desire for a good life.

The *yinyang* method

The Chinese people divide all things into *yin* 阴 and *yang* 阳. Names too have *yin* and *yang* elements. When giving a name, it is important to balance *yin* and *yang*. If a character has an odd number of strokes, it is *yang*. If the number of strokes is even, it is *yin*.

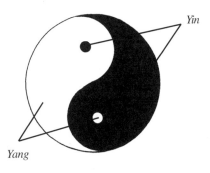

Yin

Yang

The famous *yinyang* Diagram

Let's look at the surname Wang 王. It consists of four strokes and is classified under *yin*. Fang 方, too, has four strokes and is thus categorised under *yin*. This name lacks the *yang* element.

王 方

王 芳

By adding the radical 艹 to the character 方 (*fang*), a new character 芳 (*fang*) is derived. This character consists of seven strokes and has the *yang* element. The name Wang Fang 王芳 has *yin* and *yang* elements now. It is a lucky name as the *yin* and *yang* elements are well balanced.

Elements method

The ancients believed that all things in the world were made up of the Five Elements. The Five Elements are Metal, Wood, Water, Fire and Earth. These Five Elements support and restrain one another. If the name has supporting qualities, there is balance and good fortune. Conversely, if the name has restraining qualities, it is deemed to be inauspicious.

Diagram of the Five Elements

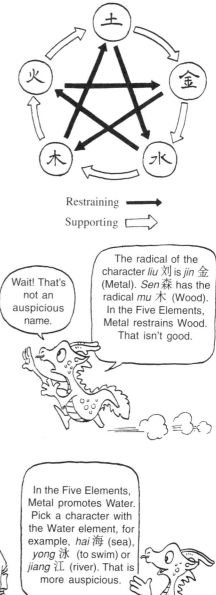

Restraining ➡

Supporting ⇨

Let's call our child 刘森 (Liu Sen).

Wait! That's not an auspicious name.

The radical of the character *liu* 刘 is *jin* 金 (Metal). *Sen* 森 has the radical *mu* 木 (Wood). In the Five Elements, Metal restrains Wood. That isn't good.

What name is auspicious then?

In the Five Elements, Metal promotes Water. Pick a character with the Water element, for example, *hai* 海 (sea), *yong* 泳 (to swim) or *jiang* 江 (river). That is more auspicious.

TYPES OF GIVEN NAMES

Zi 字 *(Name given on coming of age)*	In olden days, a second name would be given when a boy turned 20 and when a girl turned 15. For example, Kongming 孔明 was the name given to Zhuge Liang of the Three Kingdoms when he came of age. Generally, a senior will introduce himself with his *ming* 名 (first given name). A junior will address his senior or his peer by the latter's *zi*.
Hao 号 *(Nickname for adult)*	This is a name a person gives to himself. A person could have several *hao*. It could reflect his interests, physical characteristics or achievements, or it could denote the place he lives in. Examples include Arrogant One with Four Wisdoms and Master Five Willows.
Chuohao 绰号/ **Hunming** 诨名 *(Nickname)*	This nickname is given to a person based on his physical appearance. For example, in the book *All Men Are Brothers*, the character Shi Jin is called the Nine-tattoo Dragon and Wu Yong, the Resourceful Star.
Shihao 谥号 *(Honorific title given posthumously)*	In ancient times, emperors, princes, dukes and high-ranking officials were given a title based on their achievements and moral character. This title serves to commend the good and censure the evil. A title with *wen* 文 or *wu* 武 is commendatory whereas one with *li* 厉 or *you* 幽 is derogatory.
Miaohao 庙号 *(Posthumous title of deceased emperor)*	When an emperor passed away, a shrine would be constructed at the ancestral temple. He would be worshipped as one of the ancestors. Generally, if he was the founder of a dynasty, he would be given the title of Taizu 太祖, Gaozu 高祖 or Shizu 世祖 (*zu* 祖 means progenitor). The emperors who ruled after the founder were given posthumous titles such as Taizong 太宗, Shizong 世宗 or Shenzong 神宗 (*zong* 宗 means ancestor).
Nianhao 年号 *(Title of the emperor's reign)*	This is the name an emperor adopted when he ascended the throne for the purpose of keeping track of the years. Before the Ming Dynasty, an emperor could have more than one reign title. By the Ming and Qing Dynasties, most emperors had only one reign title. One example is Yongzheng. Sometimes, the reign title is used in place of the emperor's name or *miaohao*. Examples include Emperor Kangxi and Emperor Qianlong.

MARRIAGE CUSTOMS

Marriage is a significant milestone in a person's life. Chinese weddings have had many complex customs and ceremonies, many of which are still practised today.

WEDDING CEREMONY

Young Master Chen is versed in martial arts and the fine arts. He is also a man of good character.

In olden days, marriages were arranged by parents and planned by matchmakers. Children had no say at all. Preparations for a wedding began when a family sent a matchmaker to another family with a marriage proposal. The two persons' Eight Characters were then compared to see if they were compatible. The final decision lay with the parents.

Stages of a Chinese Wedding

Delivering betrothal gifts

These are betrothal presents sent by the bridegroom to the bride's family to confirm the match. Betrothal gifts include the bridal trousseau. It is a gesture made by the groom to thank the bride's parents for bringing up their daughter.

Engagement
The prospective bride and groom exchange rings, and cakes are distributed to friends and relatives to inform them of the news.

Exchanging presents
The groom's family would take presents to the bride's family. The presents usually comprise six items. It could be any six of the following: a red packet, a pair of red candles, one or more pieces of gold jewellery, pig's trotters, wine, cakes, preserved fruit, candies, chicken, bridal costume, fresh fruit, etc.

These gifts are placed on a red platter and an elderly person from the groom's family would deliver it to the bride's family. Usually, the bride's family would return some of the gifts.

Styling the hair
On the eve of the wedding, the bride and groom undergo the "styling the hair" ceremony in their respective homes. An old lady or man with a living spouse and many children and grandchildren would style the hair for the bride or groom. The ritual is performed in the hope that the newlyweds would live to a ripe old age in matrimonial bliss and have many children and grandchildren.

Overcoming sisters hurdle

The groom would be prevented by the bride's girlfriends from entering the bride's home. To cross this hurdle, the groom gives the ladies a big red packet. The two parties would haggle at the door over the amount.

Bowing to Heaven and Earth

In olden days, the bride and groom had to bow to Heaven and Earth, their parents and to each other during the wedding ceremony before they were truly considered married.

Tea ceremony

Next, the couple proceeds to the groom's place. The newlyweds then offer tea to the elders of the groom's family. By drinking the tea, the elders are showing their acceptance of the bride as a new member of the family.

The newlyweds return to the bride's home to offer tea to the elders of the bride's family. The groom will also give a roast pig, some vegetables and fruit as presents to his father-in-law. Usually, his in-laws would only accept half his gifts. The newlyweds return home with the other half.

Wedding banquet

The groom's family usually hosts a banquet after the wedding ceremony. Guests from both the groom's and the bride's families are invited. The guests give red packets to extend their good wishes.

Teasing the newlyweds in the bridal chamber

After the wedding banquet, closer friends and relatives go to the bridal chamber to play all kinds of tricks on the newlyweds. It is also a form of extending their good wishes. The practice began with the notion that fox spirits and ghosts would often appear in the bridal chamber. To drive away these spirits, there have to be many people in the bridal chamber.

Removing the veil

The bride's head is covered with a red veil. After arriving at the groom's home and having gone through the wedding ceremony, the groom removes her veil. In some places, the groom uses the beam of a steelyard or a fan to lift the veil.

Nuptial wine
The newlyweds drink the nuptial wine in the bridal chamber. They drink half a cup of wine from their own cup, then exchange cups and drink again.

Binding locks of hair
This was practised during the Song and Tang Dynasties. After the couple had drunk the nuptial wine, they snipped off a lock of their hair, and bound them together to show that they were of one heart.

Returning to the maiden home
Three, seven or nine days after the wedding, the bride pays a visit to her maiden home.

Wedding ceremony

During the Zhou Dynasty, wedding ceremonies were held at night. The groom, who wore black, would fetch the bride only when it was dark. The newlyweds' retinue and even the carriage were also in black. Those walking in front of the carriage would carry candles to light the way.

Hunli "昏"礼 refers to the meeting of *yin* and *yang*. This means that the groom (*yang*) meets the bride (*yin*). The hour of fetching the bride has to be in the night. If the auspicious hour is missed, bad luck might follow.

Interesting Marriage Customs

Woo... Mama...
Papa... take care.

Crying marriage

In some regions, two weeks to one month before the wedding ceremony, the bride will start crying in a singsong manner. The song lyrics are mostly about the sadness of parting from one's parents, brothers and sisters-in-law. Sometimes, her siblings, sisters-in-law, parents and even relatives join in the singing.

Eating half-cooked dumplings

In some regions, the bride is offered half-cooked dumplings. When the bride eats the dumplings, she would be asked: "*Sheng bu sheng?*" (生不生?) The question is a pun meaning "Is it raw?" or "Will you have babies?" If the bride answers "*Sheng*", it could mean "It's raw" or "I'd have babies".

Is it raw?
(Would you have babies?)

It's raw.
(I'd have babies.)

Carrying the bride piggyback

The custom was practised in the old days in Taiwan. On the wedding day, the groom carried the bride piggyback, and with blessings from both families, ran back to his house. On arriving, he walked round the wedding celebration venue twice before meeting his family and friends. Finally, he ran to the bridal chamber.

Red double happiness

One popular marriage custom is the pasting of the double happiness character on doors and windows. There are even embroideries of the character on pillows and blankets.

Distributing red eggs

In some places, red eggs are distributed whenever there is a marriage. Whether you are a relative or friend or even a total stranger, you can still ask the bride for a red egg.

Taboo wedding dates

Good things come in pairs. The wedding is a day of happiness for both the bride and groom. It is inauspicious to choose a date which has an odd figure. Most wedding days fall on dates with even figures. As the fifth, seventh and ninth lunar months are believed to be inauspicious, it is foolhardy to plan a wedding during these months. When a death occurs in either family, it is also unlucky to hold a wedding.

These months are not suitable for holding weddings.

Buying wedding gifts

My friend is getting married. I wish to give her a vase.

Always buy things in pairs if it's for a wedding gift. It's supposed to be a good sign. The newlyweds would be unhappy if you buy them just one vase.

Thanks for telling me. I'll buy two vases!

What will make suitable wedding gifts? Practical gifts like those that a new house will need — for example, dinner sets or curtains — are good bets.

The Origins of Teasing the Newlyweds in the Bridal Chamber

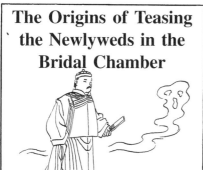

One day, Emperor Qianlong was travelling incognito.

Today is a day that brings evil luck. Why did this family choose to hold their wedding today?

There're seven evil spirits following the bridal sedan. They can wander about undetected by others but they can't escape my notice.

I'll follow them.

It's getting dark and the seven evil spirits are still waiting outside the bridal chamber. I have to do something.

According to the custom in my home village, after the wedding feast, the guests will have some fun at the bridal chamber.

This is something new. How can we have fun?

Place two tables in the bridal chamber and have some snacks, groundnuts and sweetmeat brought in. We'll ask the bride and groom to offer us the food.

Good idea! We'll all go to the bridal chamber.

A wedding is a happy occasion. We can have as much fun as we wish.

Bride, please pour us some wine.

Groom, can you sing us a song?

Cock-a-doodle-doo!

It's morning. The seven evil spirits have gone.

Time for the bride and groom to go to bed. Let's go.

The story of Emperor Qianlong driving away evil spirits by creating a disturbance in the bridal chamber spread. To ensure that the happy couple would be safe, the guests would make merry at the bridal's chamber on the wedding night. The custom is handed down to the present day.

The Origins of the Red Bridal Veil

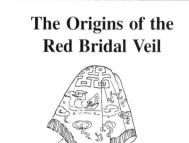

In traditional Chinese marriage customs, before the bride got into the sedan chair, she would have to cover her head with a red veil given to her by the groom's family. There is a story behind this custom.

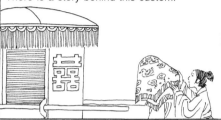

In ancient times, there was a man called Zhou Qian who was very good at predicting the future. Everyone called him Great Master Zhou.

Your son would die an unnatural death on his way home. Make preparations for his funeral.

Old Madam, why are you so sad?

Great Master Zhou said my son would die an unnatural death.

This calamity can be averted. Do as I say and I guarantee your son will return safely.

The old lady did as she was told and her son really came home safely.

Peach Blossom Girl has ruined my reputation! What a witch!

I must do something to get rid of her!

Father, I wish to marry Peach Blossom Girl. Please ask for her hand in marriage on my behalf.

All right...

Here comes my chance!

Peach Blossom Girl knew something was amiss. She decided to beat Zhou at his own game.

Young Master Zhou is quite dashing. I agree to the match.

Great Master Zhou chose an inauspicious day for the wedding. Along the way, he laid traps of stone demons and pillar spirits.

Peach Blossom Girl, you're doomed!

Sedan bearers, please drape a red cloth over all the stones and wooden signs that you see along the way.

Spirits and demons are afraid of the colour red. They will not dare to move when covered with a red cloth.

The spirits and demons also kept away from Peach Blossom Girl as she had a red cloth covering her head. The wedding ceremony went on smoothly.

She really became my daughter-in-law!

The custom of the bride wearing a red bridal veil spread. In some places, the headdress has strands of silk threads hanging down to veil the face of the bride.

64

The Origins of Fetching the Bride with a Bridal Sedan

The bridal sedan is an essential prop in a traditional marriage. The sedan chair was used as a means of transport only at the end of the Tang Dynasty and the beginning of the Five Dynasties.

Come the Northern Song Dynasty, only emperors and officials with special privileges could use the sedan chair. It was not until the Southern Song Dynasty that fetching the bride with a sedan chair became a custom.

During the reign of Emperor Song Gaozong, the Jins crossed the Yellow River and captured Bianjing. Emperor Song Gaozong crossed the Changjiang River and fled to Ningbo.

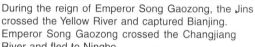

Sir, why are you so alarmed?

The Jins are after me. I have no escape.

The water here is shallow. Submerge yourself but keep your nose above the water so you can breathe.

Have you seen a man in yellow?

I saw him going that way.

When the Jins had left, the girl pulled Gaozong up and rowed him across the lake.

Two years later, Gaozong searched for the lady without any success.

Ningbo women are permitted to sit in a sedan carried by four sedan bearers when they get married.

The practice of using the sedan to fetch the bride spread to other parts of the country.

The Origins of Passing Over Bags for an Offspring

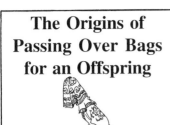

Traditionally, when the bride stepped down from the sedan chair, her feet must not touch the ground. From the sedan chair to the bridal hall, the floor must be covered with red cloth bags or straw bags and the like. This custom is known as *chuandai* 传袋 (passing over bags).

According to legend, at a wedding, two brides who looked exactly alike stepped out of the bridal sedan chair.

Who is the bride and who is the impostor?

By chance, a governor whose nickname was "Living Justice Bao" happened to pass by.

Bring me a bolt of red cloth.

Take turns to walk on the red cloth. The one who is able to make the cloth float above the ground is the real bride.

One of the brides walked across the bolt of red cloth with little difficulty. The cloth floated three inches above the ground.

When it came to the other bride's turn...

Demon woman, reveal your true form!

The bride turned into a white fox and scurried off.

Chuandai became a well-practised custom when receiving a bride.

传袋(passing over bags) and传代 (carrying on one's family name) are homophones.

Besides this custom, there were also other measures taken to stop demons and spirits from making trouble.

The bridal sedan which the groom sent to fetch the bride must not be empty. A boy would sit in the sedan so as to ward off demons and spirits. At the same time, it was a way of seeking blessings to have many sons.

When the bride got into the sedan, there was also the ritual of locking it to prevent demons from entering. Along the way, the sedan bearers had to rock the sedan chair to ward off evil spirits.

When the bride arrived at the groom's house, the matchmaker would lift the curtain of the sedan chair and use a mirror to check the interior. This is "checking the sedan with a mirror".

The Origins of Pasting the Red Double Joy Sign at Weddings

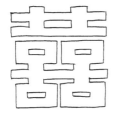

"The Jade Emperor marches with his army, The spears are the wind, the arrows are the rain, The thunder flag flashes and roars, Heaven, thou art the witness!" This makes a good couplet.

When Wang Anshi was 23, he travelled to the capital to sit for the Imperial Examination. He happened to pass by Squire Ma's place.

The first line of the couplet was put up a few months ago, and to this day, no one has been able to provide a corresponding line.

Since you find the verse excellent, please wait here for a while and I'll inform my master.

I'm sitting for the Imperial Examination tomorrow. I'll come back when I'm done with it.

In the examination hall, the Chief Examiner was impressed with Wang Anshi's talent. He sent for Wang Anshi to personally test him.

"The Dragon King gives a feast, The moon is the candle, the stars are the lanterns, The mountain drinks the sea of wine, Earth, thou art the matchmaker." Can you give a corresponding line to this?

Squire Ma's couplet corresponds to this perfectly.

This is the corresponding line: "The Jade Emperor marches with his army, The spears are the wind, the arrows are the rain, The thunder flag flashes and roars, Heaven, thou art the witness!"

Remarkable!

Wang Anshi returned to his inn after the examination.

Master Wang, you were gone in a flash. I had such a hard time tracing you here.

My master is waiting for you. Please come with me.

"The Dragon King gives a feast, The moon is the candle, the stars are the lanterns, The mountain drinks the sea of wine, Earth, thou art the matchmaker."

I have a corresponding line to the couplet.

Excellent! My daughter wrote the first line of the couplet to pick a husband. We've hung it up for six months but no one was able to give a corresponding line.

However, you've succeeded where others have failed. Couplets come in pairs and marriages bring couples together.

What do you say?

Thank you for your kindness.

Master Wang has won the honour of Top Scholar!

Congratulations! You're successful in the Imperial Examination.

Thank you.

Your ability and talent have brought you fame today. And tonight is our wedding night.

Yes, it's double happiness indeed!

Ha, ha!

A splendid couplet brings red double joy, Heaven the matchmaker, Earth the witness, Wove the silken web.

Name on the golden list on the wedding night, A small success and a huge accomplishment met.

The custom of putting up the red double happiness sign gained popularity. It became a symbol of celebration and good luck.

The Origins of Distributing Red Eggs

During the Three Kingdoms Period, Zhou Yu, governor of Eastern Wu, devised a plan for Sun Quan to re-capture the city of Jingzhou which had fallen to Liu Bei.

Master, you could pretend to betroth the princess to Liu Bei.

Zhou Yu

When Liu Bei comes down south to fetch the bride, take him hostage. He shall be returned only in exchange for Jingzhou.

Sun Quan

Sun Quan sent his men to Jingzhou to propose the match to Liu Bei. Liu Bei was hesitant as he feared it might be a plot against him.

Master, you may make the trip. I have a plan in mind. Sun Quan's sister can be yours without your having to give up Jingzhou.

Zhuge Liang

Zhuge Liang arranged for Liu Bei to take along a big vat of eggs dyed in red. On arriving at Eastern Wu, the eggs were given to everyone inside and outside the palace, regardless of rank and status.

Red eggs? What do they indicate?

Our master is going to marry the Marquis of Wu's sister.

Our master is a descendant of the imperial family. According to imperial etiquette and customs, red eggs must be distributed in a marriage. Everyone present gets a token share.

Giving out red eggs! That's a novelty.

When our children get married, we'll do the same.

Everyone now knows that Liu Bei is going to marry the princess.

If we kill him, we'll be despised. Under the circumstances, I'll have to marry the princess to Liu Bei.

Distributing red eggs at weddings became another marriage custom practised in Jiangnan. Anyone could ask for the red eggs as it was a symbol of the mythical phoenix and dragon giving blessings to the newlyweds.

Whether it's a celebration of the baby's full month, a wedding or birthday, the Chinese love to cook hard-boiled eggs, dye them red and give them to families and friends.

Symbolic Meaning of the Red Egg

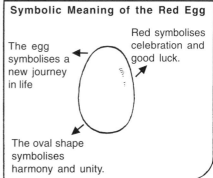

The egg symbolises a new journey in life

Red symbolises celebration and good luck.

The oval shape symbolises harmony and unity.

THE MATCHMAKER

In ancient China, no marriage could be arranged without the matchmaker. Other Asian countries like Japan and Korea have matchmakers too.

In the beginnings of the universe, there appeared a great deity whose mission was to bring together all men and women under Heaven. Can you guess who this deity is?

Matchmaking

In ancient China, marriage was arranged through the will of one's parents and the words of a matchmaker. The matchmaker is the go-between. A man would not take a wife without the matchmaker and a woman would not marry without the go-between. Marital knots that were tied without the matchmaker were derided.

Matchmakers can be divided into three categories: the Goddess of Marriage, the marriage official and the go-between.

Goddess of Marriage
The Goddess of Marriage is Nüwa. Legend has it that she moulded Man from yellow earth.

To ensure that the humankind would flourish, she brought men and women together so they would have children.

With this legend, Nüwa was worshipped as the Goddess of Marriage. Temples and shrines were built in her name. Every year, sacrificial offerings of three animals — the pig, ox and goat — would be placed at these temples.

So the world's first matchmaker is Nüwa!

Marriage official

In ancient times, there existed a bureau that was in charge of marriages. It is similar to our modern marriage bureau. Under special circumstances, the government would appoint a marriage official.

During the Zhou Dynasty, the marriage official was fully in charge of the marriages of thousands of people. He kept a register of single men and women and set the rules of marriage. He would decide the legal marriageable age, handle marital disputes, determine the best season to hold weddings, punish those who held a wedding outside the stipulated season, help widows and widowers to rebuild a family, and allot farming land and houses.

Go-between

The go-between is a professional matchmaker. Arranging marriages as an occupation goes as far back as the late Zhou Dynasty. Even today, there are professionals who arrange matches. With the gift of the gab, the matchmaker is like a broker shuttling between two parties. Naturally, the credibility of the matchmaker plays a major role in the success of a marriage.

Most matchmakers were women of middle age or older, hence the term "*meipo* 媒婆", where *mei* means matchmaker and *po*, old lady. Male matchmakers are rare. But it was said that the first matchmaker in China was an old man.

The Origins of the Matchmaker

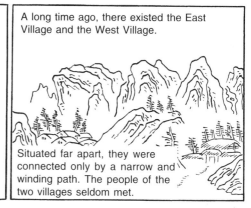

A long time ago, there existed the East Village and the West Village.

Situated far apart, they were connected only by a narrow and winding path. The people of the two villages seldom met.

Later, Zhao Jing, a young man from the East Village, married Cai, a girl from the West Village, through an old man's arrangement.

They were a loving and devoted couple.

It's strange. We were perfect strangers in the past.

But the kind old man brought us together and we became husband and wife.

We owe our happy marriage to him and should repay him.

But he's left. Where can we find him?

Three Matchmakers and Six Items of Proof

In a traditional Chinese marriage, the match is not confirmed until the engagement ritual is sealed with "three matchmakers and six items of proof".

What are the three match-makers and six items of proof? The following story tells their origins.

Long, long ago, there were three brothers. All of them were *xiucai**. They were nicknamed "Zhuge's Rivals****". One day, they teased Squire Luo.

Squire Luo, you're a charitable man, but can you donate grains as much as the ocean waters, ...

... fabric as long as the rainbow and buns that pile up as tall as mountains?

Er...

That's not difficult. But I'll need six items of proof. When you've brought me the items, my father will donate what you've asked for.

Every family has these items. If you can't find them in three days, don't ever call yourselves Zhuge's Rivals.

Six items of proof? What are they?

*Xiucai 秀才 were scholars who had passed the Imperial Examination at the county level.
** Here, Zhuge refers to Zhuge Liang 诸葛亮, a brilliant military tactician during the Three Kingdoms Period.

The three scholars asked around but no one could tell them what the six items of proof were, until...

Ha! You've been tricked by Young Master Luo.

Three days later...

Squire Luo, we've brought the six items of proof. To weigh grains, I have brought a *sheng** and an abacus. To weigh buns, there's the steelyard.

For measuring and cutting cloth, I have the ruler and scissors. The mirror gives proof of a person's appearance.

Correct! But did you come up with the answer yourselves?

To tell you the truth, a girl in our neighbourhood told us the answer.

What a clever girl!

Can the three of you play matchmaker for my son? What betrothal gifts should we offer her?

With the six items of proof and us, the three matchmakers, she will certainly become your daughter-in-law.

Ha, ha! Indeed, what do I have to worry about?

After this incident, people would engage three matchmakers and the bride's family would prepare six items of proof as confirmation of the betrothal. This custom eventually spread to other places.

*Sheng 升 is a vessel for measuring weight.

God of Marriage — Old Man Under the Moon

During the Tang Dynasty, there was a man named Wei Gu. One night, he encountered an old man.

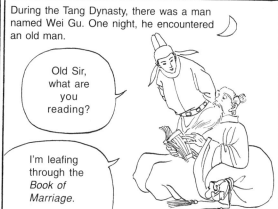

Old Sir, what are you reading?

I'm leafing through the *Book of Marriage*.

Book of Marriage? Is there such a book?

And what is in your bag?

Even if they're enemies, far apart in social status and living in different corners of the world, once the thread is tied, their destinies are bound together forever.

Red threads for tying the feet of married couples.

Can you check whom I'll marry?

Your fiancée is the three-year-old daughter of a blind lady who sells vegetables.

What? I can't marry a vegetable-seller's daughter!

He secretly sent his servant to kill the girl, but she was only injured in her forehead. Wei Gu and his servant fled in the dark.

Some 10 years later, Wei Gu, who had joined the army, proved himself to be a brave soldier. Governor Wang Tai was impressed and betrothed his daughter to him.

My dear, why do you always wear a flower sticker on your forehead?

I have a scar there. When I was young, I was wounded in the forehead.

As she related the story, Wei Gu realised that she was the little girl he had tried to harm more than 10 years ago. The governor had adopted her and had been treating her like his own.

The will of Heaven cannot be defied. Our marriage was long decided by Heaven.

Their children grew up to be very successful. They had many grandchildren and led a happy life.

BIRTH CUSTOMS

The arrival of a new life is often cause for joy. And to be able to live to a ripe old age is also reason to celebrate. The Chinese people have a range of joyous customs to mark the significant milestones in a person's life from birth till old age.

CUSTOMS OF PRAYING FOR CHILDREN

The Chinese have this saying: Of the three unfilial acts, the worst is the failure to produce children. Childbearing is a duty that is given a strong moral tone.

To have many children and grandchildren is good fortune.

With this eagerness to have offspring, many customs linked with praying to the gods for children grew in popularity.

Praying to deities

The most direct way was to seek blessings from the gods of birth. For instance, people worship the deity Zhang Xian, Goddess of Offspring, Queen Mother Golden Flower, Goddess of Mercy, Queen Mother of Births and Goddess Guizi.

Consuming wedding eggs

Another custom was to consume wedding eggs. For the Chinese, the dowry often includes a "children bucket" painted in red. In the bucket, there would be five hard-boiled eggs dyed in red and some fortune sweetmeat. When the dowry was delivered to the groom's house, female relatives of the groom's family who did not have children even after a long marriage could ask for these red eggs. It was said they would conceive after eating it.

Eating melons

Interestingly, some places practised the custom of eating melons to get a child. Usually, the melons refer to either the pumpkin or the white gourd. The trailing stems and leaves of the pumpkin are lush. On its joints sprout roots. A single plant could bear many pumpkins. Moreover, the *nan* in *nangua* 南瓜 (pumpkin) and *nan* 男 (male) are homophones. Among the different types of melons, the white gourd contains the most seeds. It is sometimes known as the "vat of 100 seeds" (seeds implying children).

Legend has it that a couple with no son should buy a pumpkin on the "actual Qingming Day". They are to cook the whole pumpkin and eat it at noon. Seated side by side, the couple should finish as much of the pumpkin as possible. With that done, they would have children before long.

Zhang Xian the Child-giving Deity

Zhang Xian is the only male God of Birth. It is said that Zhang Xian was Emperor Meng Chang of the Five Dynasties.

After defeating Emperor Meng Chang, Emperor Song Taizu took away Meng Chang's beloved concubine Huarui.

Madam Huarui missed her husband and drew a picture of Meng Chang drawing a bow in a hunting posture. She hung the picture in her chamber.

The story spread to the common folk and women began hanging up pictures of Zhang Xian and praying to him for children.

Who is this?

Deity Zhang Xian, the child-giver. Back home, we pray to him to bless us with children.

He has a marble in his right hand. Marble (*dan* 弹) is pronounced in the same way as birth (诞).

Legend has it that the Heavenly Dog would wriggle into the house through the chimney to scare children and spread smallpox. With Zhang Xian around, the Heavenly Dog would not dare to enter.

The five boys symbolise five achievements.

Zhang Xian holds a bow in his left hand.

Picture of Zhang Xian the child-giver

Delivering Stolen Melons to Childless Couples

On the night of the 15th day of the eighth lunar month, children would group together to steal pumpkins or white gourds from the fields.

They drew the face of a child on the pumpkin. Then, carrying lanterns and beating on drums and cymbals, they presented these melons to newlyweds and childless couples.

The children walked directly into the bedroom, put the melon on the bed and covered it with a blanket.

Even if the melon was smudged with mud and dirtied the blankets, a family which longed for a child would not get upset. Instead, they would extend their warmest hospitality to the young melon-deliverers. If a couple who received a melon really had a child, they would give presents to the kid who had delivered the melon.

The Child-giving Unicorn

Of the four great mythical animals — the Unicorn, Dragon, Phoenix and Tortoise — the Chinese rank the Unicorn first. It is said that the Unicorn would give children to childless families who had done good deeds.

The birth of Confucius, the famous sage, is said to be related to the tale of the child-giving Unicorn.

Before Confucius was born, his father Shu Lianghe already had seven children. However, the only son he had walked with a limp.

Later, Shu Lianghe married the young Yan Zhengzai. After many years, she still did not conceive. The couple went to Mt Ni to pray for a son.

89

One night, after the couple had offered prayers…

Everyone, come take a look! It's the Unicorn!

This is a good sign! Look, he's spat out a piece of silk cloth.

"The finest of the finest, in clothes plain, he's wise and brilliant."

He must be bringing a son to a family. That child will be a brilliant boy.

The neigbours tied a colourful sash to the Unicorn's horn to thank him.

A sage is going to be born in our village!

The Unicorn disappeared the next day, and cries of a baby were heard in Shu Lianghe's house. Confucius was born.

Later, at Confucius' hometown, Qufu, a farmer who was tilling the land dug up the colourful sash that was tied to the Unicorn's horn.

ONE-MONTH CONFINEMENT PERIOD

Chinese women observe the one-month confinement period after giving birth. This is a custom unique to the Chinese and has been practised for a long time, even today. Within a month after giving birth, a woman has to take special care of herself by keeping warm, reducing air in the stomach and taking tonics. An old adage says: Follow the rules of the confinement and be freed of worries all your life. How much rest a woman gets during her month-long confinement period is crucial as it can affect her physical health in future.

Removing wind: Stay away from the wind. Do not wash hair, bathe, touch cold water or go out.

Keeping warm: Wear long-sleeved clothes, long pants and socks.

✔

Taking tonics: Tonics like chicken wine, chicken cooked in sesame oil, greasy glutinous rice, millet gruel, hard-boiled eggs, chicken clear soup, salted sesame, walnut kernel and black sugar are recommended. This is to replenish blood lost during childbirth and, at the same time, ensure that the mother would have abundant milk to nurse the baby.

✗

Abstaining from cold and raw food: Avoid fruit and vegetables like watermelon, pears, spinach and Chinese cabbage.

CUSTOMS OF BRINGING UP CHILDREN

Congratulations! You've got a son!

Full-month celebrations

On the baby's full month, some families host a dinner to entertain friends and relatives. Red hard-boiled eggs will be distributed too.

An odd number of eggs will be distributed if it is a boy and an even number of eggs if it is a girl. Friends and relatives usually give a red packet in return. They may also give presents like baby food, articles for daily use or jewellery.

Shaving baby's hair

The Chinese also practise the custom of shaving off the baby's hair on its full month.

The baby's hair is wrapped up in a red cloth and sewn to the baby's pillow. It seems that by doing this, the baby would not be timid or easily frightened.

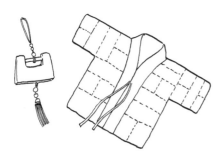

100-year-old ceremony

A hundred days after the baby's birth, the 100-year-old ceremony would be held. *Bai* 百 (hundred) connotes complete satisfaction. The usual gifts are the 100-family lock and the 100-family robe. They symbolise longevity.

Accessories

Parents love to give their children earrings* and anklets. These pieces of jewellery are believed to be punishment tools used by the gods. By wearing them, the child would have the protection of the deities. Some parents engrave the names of gods or words like longevity, wealth and fortune on the jewellery to ensure that the child will have a long life. When the child grows up, the parents will remove the jewellery.

Giving the child a humble name is popular among common folks. It is to ensure that the child will grow to maturity. Examples of such names are Doggie, Potato, Beggar, Dog and Ox. In the north, boys are given a girl's name. Many boys are called Girl or Wench and wear one earring.

I'm a boy. Why does Mother call me Girl and make me wear an earring? It's so awkward.

Girl, come have your meal!

The Chinese Notion of Age

In the traditional Chinese way of counting age, a child is one year old the moment he's born. A year is added to his age each lunar new year. This is his nominal age.

That makes the child one or two years older than his true age.

Wow, that's fast ageing!

Earrings are mostly made of gold or silver and anklets, mostly silver, bronze or iron.

Giving the Child a Repulsive Name

Giving the child a repulsive name actually embodies the love of the parents for their child.

Read the following story and you'll know why.

Long ago, there was a peasant who named his son Baby Ox.

One day, King Yama gave an order to his hell guard.

Find a little boy to sacrifice to our ancestors.

The hell guard caught Baby Ox and took him to the Court of Yama.

What's your name?

Baby Ox.

A Vocational Inclination Test for the Child

In olden days, when a child turned one, some families would test the child to see his inclination. Items like the bow, arrow, paper and brush (for girls, it'd be replaced with scissors, ruler, needle and thread) and all kinds of little treasures, foodstuff and toys were placed in a basin. The basin would be placed before the child.

Whatever the child picked would be used to predict his future. Is this an accurate method? Let's see the story below and you decide for yourself.

There's much disagreement as to whom I should pick as the crown prince. Is there a solution to this?

During the Three Kingdoms Period, Sun Quan's son Sun Deng, who was the crown prince, died of an illness. There was a struggle for the position among the other princes.

Who you appoint as your successor will have far-reaching effects on the state. That he is moral and kind is not good enough. The qualities that his son possesses are critical too.

Jing Yang

I have a way to test the benevolence and intelligence of the princes' sons.

Taking Jing Yang's advice, Sun Quan picked an auspicious day and ordered his princes to bring their children to the palace for a test. All the officials came to watch. Jing Yang took out a big platter filled with conches, pearls, ivory, rhino horns, books, ribbons and other articles.

The children grabbed the items that caught their eyes. Some took pieces of jade, some the ivory. Only Sun Hao, Sun He's son, took the bamboo scroll and the ribbon.

Ha ha... You're my good grandchild.

Good! I'll make you my crown prince.

But the other princes objected. Sun Quan gave in and named Sun Liang as his successor. Three years after Sun Liang ascended the throne, he was forced to abdicate in favour of his elder brother Sun Xiu. However, Sun Xiu died after seven years as the emperor.

The ministers then nominated Sun Hao as the successor. Some old officials recalled the day the infants were taken to the palace for the inclination test and were surprised at the strange coincidence.

The story spread and the vocational inclination test became a custom.

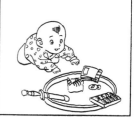

BIRTHDAYS AND BIRTHDAY BANQUETS

Everyone has a birthday. In Chinese traditional thinking, only a person who is 60 years old or older has the privilege of celebrating his birthday.

A person below the age of 60 should not celebrate his birthday in a big way as this may cut short his life!

Why is this so? In Chinese thought, the Heavenly Stems and Earthly Branches make a full circle in 60 years. Those who are 60 would have completed this full cycle so they are no ordinary people. They enjoy the same respect shown to the ancestors. On their birthdays, their children and grandchildren would extend their best wishes to them.

The numbers 9 and 10 are important in these celebrations. The best number is 9 as it connotes the very best and also sounds like the word for eternity. Thus, when a person's age has a number 9 or if the age is a multiple of 9, a big celebration would be planned. This is known as the celebration of 9. The number 10 is regarded as a complete whole and ages in figures of tens are known as "complete whole birthdays". A person who has reached 80 is looked upon as an old star-god. His birthday celebration would be a big bash.

The Chart of the 60-year cycle

1	甲子	2	乙丑	3	丙寅	4	丁卯	5	戊辰	6	己巳	7	庚午	8	辛未	9	壬申	10	癸酉
11	甲戌	12	乙亥	13	丙子	14	丁丑	15	戊寅	16	己卯	17	庚辰	18	辛巳	19	壬午	20	癸未
21	甲申	22	乙酉	23	丙戌	24	丁亥	25	戊子	26	己丑	27	庚寅	28	辛卯	29	壬辰	30	癸巳
31	甲午	32	乙未	33	丙申	34	丁酉	35	戊戌	36	己亥	37	庚子	38	辛丑	39	壬寅	40	癸卯
41	甲辰	42	乙巳	43	丙午	44	丁未	45	戊申	46	己酉	47	庚戌	48	辛亥	49	壬子	50	癸丑
51	甲寅	52	乙卯	53	丙辰	54	丁巳	55	戊午	56	己未	57	庚申	58	辛酉	59	壬戌	60	癸亥

How Do We Celebrate Birthday?

Main hall

The main hall must be decorated if the birthday celebration is held at home. Paste a big poster with the character *shou* 寿 (birthday) on the wall. Hang up colourful curtains and light red candles. Next, treat invited guests to a sumptuous feast. Most guests will bring two to four gifts. These range from eggs, birthday noodles, birthday peaches, gifts, wine, red packets to birthday banners (cloth bearing inscriptions of poems or blessings) and birthday couplets.

Longevity wine

Among foodstuff given as gifts, *jiu* 酒 wine is the most common as it sounds like 久 (which connotes longevity). To offer wine is to wish the person longevity. All wines are referred to as birthday wines. It can be osmanthus wine, green wine, scholar wine or ginseng wine.

Longevity noodles

Young or old, everyone takes longevity noodles on his or her birthday. When cooking the noodles, care must be taken not to cut the strands.

The custom began when it was said that Pengzu, who had a long face, lived to be 800 years old. *Mianchang* 面长 is a pun on the expressions "a long face" and "long strands of noodles". By eating long strands of noodles, it is hoped that one would live as long as Pengzu.

Birthday peaches

Birthday peaches are also a must. In Chinese mythology, birthday peaches are produced through the passing of time and contain the essence of the sun and moon. Eating the peaches would prolong life. As fresh peaches are not available all year round, they are replaced by flour peaches.

Birthday feast

Wearing new clothes, the protagonist would sit in the centre of the hall to receive the wishes of his family and guests. If the person extending birthday wishes is of the same generation, he would stand up to show his respect. For the kids whose parents belong to a younger generation, he gives them red packets. After the ceremony, the feast begins.

In some places, gifts are distributed to guests. It means returning home with the good fortune of living as long as the old birthday boy.

The Chinese have this saying: An aged person is a jewel in his family. Old people have a wealth of experience and it is experience that brings wisdom. They are like a magic box with an inexhaustible supply of treasures.

Celebrating the birthdays of old folks is the younger generation's way of showing filial piety and respect.

The Origins of Birthday Celebrations

Long time ago, an emperor believed that a person who had reached the age of 60 would no longer do any productive work and would, instead, become a burden. It prompted him to pass a decree.

Execute all those who have reached the age of 60.

Father is 59. What should I do?

I'll hide him in a cave and take food to him every day.

One day, an emissary from a small state presented two pieces of wood of the same thickness.

If you can differentiate the branch from the root, we will pay tribute to your country every year.

If you can't differentiate them, we'll sever all ties.

None of the court officials could tell the two pieces of wood apart.

Anyone who succeeds will be rewarded with 1,000 pieces of silver.

When the official delivered food to his father, he told him what had happened.

Place the pieces of wood in the water. The root is heavier and will sink. The branch is lighter and will float.

The official told the emperor this method. They finally succeeded in differentiating the root from the branch.

Since you're able to differentiate them, our state will keep our promise and continue to pay tribute to your country.

A year later, the same emissary came and presented two gold coins of exactly the same size. But one was made of gold while the other was made of bronze.

If you can tell which is a real gold coin, we'll send yearly tribute to you. Otherwise, we'll sever all ties.

Whoever can tell the difference will be rewarded with 20,000 pieces of gold.

Again, the court officials were stumped.

The official sought his father's advice once more.

Use a balance to weigh the coins. Gold is heavier than bronze, so you'll be able to tell the difference.

The official followed his father's instructions and succeeded in differentiating the two coins. The emissary had to submit once again.

You're a brilliant man. I'll make you the premier.

I've committed a crime. Please punish me.

It's with my father's help that I was able to solve those two difficult problems.

I thought old people were useless. I could not be more wrong. No youngster can be compared to the elderly who are more experienced and wiser.

The emperor personally paid the old man a visit.

The next day, the emperor gave a feast to show his appreciation. Coincidentally, it was the old man's 60th birthday. The emperor bowed to him three times and even wanted to go down on his knees.

I accept your bows but I cannot let you kneel to me.

Since then, a birthday banquet would be held for a person who has reached 60 years of age as a show of filial piety.

壽

The Origins of Birthday Cakes and Peaches

When an old person celebrates his birthday, his children, relatives and friends would offer him gifts and wish him good health, longevity and happiness. Most of the gifts are cakes and peaches made of flour.

The custom first grew in popularity during the Warring States Period. At Mt Yunmeng, famous war strategist Sun Bin became a disciple of Guiguzi. To master the art of war, he did not return home for 12 years.

It's Mother's 80th birthday today.

Even animals know how to return kindness. Yet, for 12 years, I did not repay my mother for her care and concern.

Master, I wish to visit my mother.

Take this peach to your mother to wish her well.

Madam, Third Young Master has returned.

Mother, it's your 80th birthday. I've returned specially to extend birthday wishes to you. This is a peach from my master.

This peach is so fragrant and sweet.

Mother, your hair has turned dark and your wrinkles have disappeared.

Ah, yes! I can see better now and new teeth have grown too.

Madam, you've become much younger after taking the divine peach.

When the story spread, children started to present peaches to their parents on their birthdays. It was a wish that they would lead long and healthy lives.

Being a seasonal fruit, the peach is not available in winter, spring and early summer. That is why flour is used to make birthday peaches. The peaches are presented only after they have been steamed. This is still practised today.

107

THE 12 ANIMAL SIGNS

If you wish to ask a Chinese friend his age but do not want to seem too direct, subtly pose the question in this way:

"What is your animal sign?" From his animal sign, you can make a good guess of his age.

What are the 12 animal signs? This brings us back to the 10 Heavenly Stems and 12 Earth Branches mentioned in the last chapter. Do you still remember them? The Heavenly Stems and Earthly Branches form a system that designates years.

The 12 animal signs are paired with the 12 Earthly Branches. The 12 animal signs are arranged in this order: Rat, Ox, Tiger, Rabbit, Dragon, Snake, Horse, Goat, Monkey, Rooster, Dog and Pig.

子 Zi

丑 Chou

寅 Yin

卯 Mao

辰 Chen

巳 Si

午 Wu

未 Wei

申 Shen

酉 You

戌 Xu

亥 Hai

Animal Signs and Astrology

By the Eastern Zhou Dynasty, the 12 animals were linked to the year in which one was born. They became the 12 animal signs. When a Chinese baby is born, the animal sign of that year would be his animal sign. For example, those born in 1998 are tigers and those born in the year 2000 are dragons.

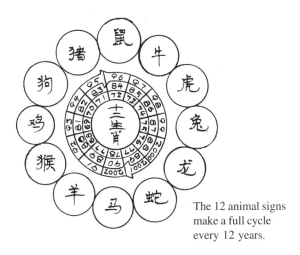

The 12 animal signs make a full cycle every 12 years.

Predicting One's Fortunes

At first, the 12 animal signs were used to denote years. It later developed into a system for predicting one's fortune.

We share the same animal sign, yet our fortunes are poles apart.

I have always lived in plenty because I was born under a good animal sign.

Those born in spring or summer in the year of the goat will always live in comfort. But those born in autumn and winter will always be poor and have to work hard for a living.

Marriage partners could be picked based on the compatibility and conflicting nature of their animal signs.

It is good for the hen and ox to be together.

The goat and the tiger are incompatible. It is as good as "delivering the goat right into the tiger's mouth".

There are more taboos linked to the tiger than other animal signs. For example, it is best to avoid asking women born in the year of the tiger to be bridesmaids. This is to avoid frightening away the God of Glad Tidings.

Among the 12 animal signs, the dragon, that's me, is the most popular. All parents hope that their children will become dragons, which symbolise great achievements.

Not everyone born in the year of the dragon will be successful. Still, more babies are born in the year of the dragon than in any other year.

Animal signs are not unique to China. Some other countries have 12 animal signs too. Let's look at the similarities and differences.

Comparisons of Animal Signs

China	India	Egypt	Babylon	Thailand	Cambodia
Rat	Rat	Bull	Cat	Snake	Ox
Ox	Ox	Mountain	Dog	Horse	Tiger
Tiger	Lion	goat	Snake	Goat	Rabbit
Rabbit	Rabbit	Lion	Dung	Monkey	Dragon
Dragon	Dragon	Donkey	beetle	Rooster	Snake
Snake	Snake	Crab	Donkey	Dog	Horse
Horse	Horse	Snake	Lion	Pig	Goat
Goat	Goat	Dog	Ram	Rat	Monkey
Monkey	Monkey	Cat	Bull	Ox	Rooster
Rooster	Rooster	Crocodile	Falcon	Tiger	Dog
Dog	Dog	Scarlet ibis	Monkey	Rabbit	Pig
Pig	Pig	Ape	Crocodile	Dragon	Rat
		Eagle	Scarlet ibis		

Strange! Why isn't the cat included in the 12 animal signs?

Yes, and why is the rat placed first? Shouldn't it be me, the dragon?

All right, quiet! Read on and you will know why.

People born under different animal signs have different personalities. These signs are similar to the 12 horoscopes of the West.

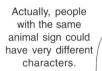

Actually, people with the same animal sign could have very different characters.

There is no need to take all this too seriously.

Animal Signs	Personality Traits	Famous Personalities Born Under the Signs
Rat	Adaptable and skilful at securing personal gains but lacks patience	Guan Yu, Su Dongpo, Bai Juyi, Du Fu, Wolfgang Amadeus Mozart, William Shakespeare, George Washington,
Ox	Honest and hardworking but stubborn; also tends to waste time and effort over insignificant issues	Liu Zongyuan, Qiu Jin, Zhang Xueliang, Wang Luobin, Adolf Hitler, Charlie Chaplin, Napoleon Bonaparte, Hans Christian Anderson, Vincent Van Gogh
Tiger	Highly confident and will go all out to attain his goal but can be rather self-centred	Qu Yuan, Emperor Qin Shihuang, Zhang Heng, Tang Bohu, Li Shizhen, Shi Kefa, Sun Yat-sen, Marco Polo, Karl Marx
Rabbit	Gentle, intelligent, and neat but can be indecisive and conservative	Zhou Yu, Cao Pi, Emperor Qianlong, Hu Shi, Albert Einstein
Dragon	A decisive risk-taker with leadership qualities	Zhu Yuanzhang, Huo Yuanjia, Wang Yangming, Buddhist Master Hongyi, Bruce Lee, George Bernard Shaw
Snake	Adaptable, cool-headed and sharp, but can be rather cold and distant	Xiang Yu, Kong Rong, Lin Zexu, Lu Xun, Mao Zedong, Abraham Lincoln, Mahatma Gandhi, Pablo Picasso

Xu Beihong

Zhang Daqian

Qi Baishi

Confucius

Animal Signs	Personality Traits	Famous Personalities Born Under the Signs
Horse	Independent, positive and full of enthusiasm, but cannot keep secrets	Li Shimin, Genghis Khan, Emperor Kangxi, Pu Yi, Vladmir Ilyich Lenin
Goat	Persevering and down-to-earth but conservative and averse to change	Cao Cao, Yang Guifei, Yue Fei, Empress Dowager Cixi, Xu Beihong, Mark Twain, Thomas Edison
Monkey	Adaptable and quick-witted but restless and lacks foresight	Empress Wu Zetian, Han Yu, Wen Tianxiang, Liu Haisu, Julius Caesar, Leonardo da Vinci
Rooster	Serious and has foresight but too proud as well as impatient	Confucius, Emperor Han Wudi, Zhuge Liang, Wang Anshi, Zheng Banqiao, Rabindranath Tagore
Dog	Loyal and observant but temperamental as well as impatient	Xuanzang, Xu Xiaoke, Tan Kah Kee, Zhu Ziqing
Pig	Born leader, determined but stubborn and egoistic	Emperor Song Taizu, Liu Bowen, Qi Baishi, Zhang Daqian, Shi Huaizhe, Henry Ford

Story of the 12 Animal Signs

The Jade Emperor wanted to choose 12 animals to oversee the hours of the day.

There are so many animals in the world. How should I pick them?

Let them take part in a race.

The 12 fastest animals will be selected.

The animals were very excited and kept talking about the event.

The cat and the rat were very good friends then.

Buddy, I'm going to take a nap. Wake me up before the race.

No problem.

When the race started, the rat had clean forgotten the cat's request.

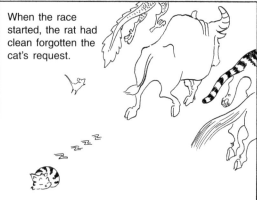

The ox is the fastest. Let me hitch a ride.

Ha ha! I'm first!

Finishing Point

The rat is first, the ox second, followed by the tiger, rabbit, dragon, snake and so on. That will be the sequence of the 12 animal signs.

Why didn't you wake me up?

That's just an interesting tale. It isn't really the rat's fault that the cat isn't among the 12 animal signs.

Way back in those days when the 12 animal signs were created, there were no cats in China. Cats appeared in China only during the Eastern Zhou Dynasty. That is why the cat is not on the list.

The cat was so angry that he regarded the rat as an enemy. Since then, the rat will run away whenever he sees the cat.

115

The pig is thought to be lazy and greedy. No wonder he's placed last in the 12 animal signs.

But the pig is said to be smart. In fact, he is as clever as the dog.

The Last Animal Sign — The Pig

There was a wealthy landlord who had a son only when he was almost 60. On the day of the baby's full month, he asked the fortune-teller to read his son's fortunes.

The son grew up thinking he was born to have a good life and did not have to work for a living.

Your son has the features of a man who will grow prosperous. He'll become very rich.

Young Master, you should be studying.

Whatever for? I am born to lead a good life. Even if I don't study, I'll grow rich.

117

DEATH CUSTOMS

For the Chinese, both birth and death are events that call for a big gathering of people. A baby's full month is celebrated. When a person grows old, his birthday is celebrated. When he dies, there are complicated rituals to observe. Some old people even make arrangements for their funerals beforehand.

FUNERAL PREPARATIONS

What kind of wood should I pick?

Choosing the wood for the coffin

Once the wood is chosen, it is put away and must not be moved again. It is believed ill fortune will befall the person if the rule is not followed. The drier the wood, the better, as it means the person will have fewer sicknesses in his next life.

I'm getting on in years. Better get my robe ready.

Tailoring the longevity robe

The robe has to be put on before a person breathes his last. Therefore, it has to be tailored beforehand.

The *fengshui* here is good. If you're buried here, your descendants will become high-ranking officials.

Erecting the tomb

Construction of the tomb is another preparation. The rich will usually engage a geomancer to choose the burial ground. It is believed that the *fengshui* 风水 of the tomb can affect the future of later generations.

The funeral

When one's parents or elders pass away, one will usually try one's best to arrange a decent funeral. "Be filial to your elders when they are alive and mourn their passing when they die" is a Confucian teaching on filial piety.

Keeping vigil beside the coffin can last from three to seven days. According to customs, it has to be an odd number of days as an even number of days implies a happy occasion.

The funeral wake

During the funeral, the body is placed in the mourning hall for relatives and friends to pay their last respects.

Visitors bring wreaths, banners with elegiac couplets written on them and cash contributions placed in white envelopes.

The bereaved family distributes red threads or red packets, each containing a coin, to friends and relatives so that they would return home safely.

When you attend a funeral wake, avoid wearing anything colourful. Wear sombre colours to show respect for the bereaved family.

Burning joss paper

The Chinese believe there is a netherworld. To enable their loved ones to live comfortably in the netherworld, well-to-do families burn paper cars, paper houses, paper TV sets and even paper maids.

The funeral procession

At the end of the final overnight vigil, the coffin is carried to the burial ground or the crematorium. A band usually leads the funeral procession. The music is meant to frighten away ghosts and spirits that might be lurking around. The cortege forms behind. The sons and daughters make up the first row, followed by other members of the family. Step by step, they walk to the graveyard.

The mourning period

In ancient China, children were required to mourn for three years after their parents' deaths. During the mourning period, singing and dancing were forbidden and men were not to take wives or concubines. Wine and meat were to be abstained. The sons even had to build a hut beside the grave and live there. At the end of the third year, a grand ceremony during which rites were performed was held. This would mark the end of the mourning period.

Mourning clothes

The family members wear mourning clothes. The different colours of the mourning clothes show the relationship the living had with the deceased. Sons, daughters and daughters-in-law wear black and white. Grandsons and granddaughters wear blue.

Mourning band

The small piece of cloth pinned on the sleeve is known as the mourning band. This shows that the person wearing it is in mourning. If the person who has passed away is a man, the band is pinned on the left sleeve. If the deceased is a woman, the band is pinned on the right sleeve. The mourning band is usually won for 49 to 100 days.

During the mourning period and the period when the mourning band is worn, mourners must wear sombre colours. Colourful clothes are avoided.

Ancient burial customs

During the reign of Shun, baked clay coffins were used to bury the dead. By the time of Yu of the Xia Dynasty, people were using baked bricks to build tombs within which dead bodies could be placed.

During the Shang Dynasty, the practice of using coffins began. By then, a class system of tombs had emerged. The kind of tomb and the articles buried with the deceased depended on his status. There were also specifications on how the tomb should be built.

Imperial tombs

During the Spring and Autumn Period, trees were planted beside tombs. Then came the practice of sealing off hills to build tombs. For example, the tomb of Qin Shihuang is as high as a mountain range.

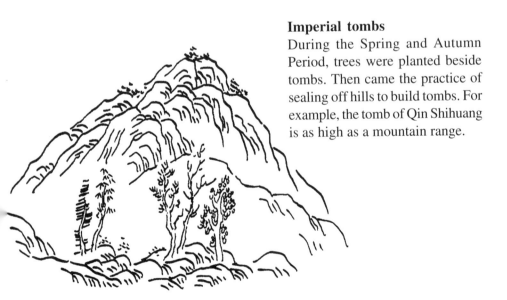

Burial objects

The tombs of emperors, the nobility, ministers and high-ranking officials had underground palaces. All sorts of valuable sculptures, paintings and rare treasures were buried with them.

The 7,000-odd terracotta warriors that Emperor Qin Shihuang was buried with are life-sized models of men and horses. They are so lifelike that they have been touted as the "Eighth Wonder of the World".

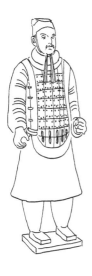 

Commoners' burial

Commoners buried the dead by placing the bodies in wooden coffins. Ancient books have records of poor folks selling themselves to raise money to bury their parents. This shows that the early Chinese people considered it important to give the dead a decent burial.

Wearing Mourning Clothes

During the Spring and Autumn Period, the great thinker Confucius, who advocated ethical ideals like filial piety, loyalty, righteousness and honour, taught his students to respect and be filial to their elders.

A disciple of one of Confucius' followers became an official. He strongly promoted Confucius' teachings, especially filial piety.

Sir, you truly honour and respect the elderly.

Unfortunately, we still see unfilial acts.

I must find a way to compel people to be filial to their elders.

Each time an old person died in the family, the official would gather the neighbours and relatives. They were to give their frank opinions as to which son had been most filial to the deceased.

The filial one would be hailed as a filial son. His uncles and aunts would contribute some money to make a white robe and a white hat for him. The son would also be entitled to the inheritance.

It's a good move! More and more people are showing respect for their parents.

No one considers me a filial son. I have no right to the inheritance and am too ashamed to see anyone.

I'll make the mourning clothes and the hat myself.

The custom of wearing mourning clothes spread, but the practice of judging whether the son was filial or not died out. However, it became customary for the younger generation to wear mourning clothes when an elder in the family had passed away. This custom is still practised today.

Burning Joss Paper for the Dead

Scholar You learnt the technique of making paper under Cai Lun.

My dear, what is troubling you?

I'm good at making paper, but I've not been able to sell it as few people use paper.

Three days later...

Sob... sob...

Who has passed away in the You family?

It's Scholar You.

Sob... The family is poor and there is nothing we can bury with him.

I'll burn the paper that he made as offerings to him.

Scholar You's family burnt the paper before his altar.

Burn the paper! Burn the paper!

Three days later...

128

THE ANCESTRAL TABLET

Besides the gods, the Chinese also worship their ancestors.

The ancestral tablets reflect the practice of ancestral worship.

The Chinese believe there is a soul and a body. When a person dies, his soul will rise to the Heavens whereas his body will remain on Earth. Though his body is dead, his soul still exists.

It is believed that the soul can never be destroyed. The living can communicate with and seek blessings from the soul. But one can only pray to the souls of the ancestors only if there is a resting place for them. Tablets serve this purpose. Eventually, ancestral tablets are made.

As most tablets are made of wood, they are sometimes referred to as the masters of wood. The eldest son or eldest grandson has the responsibility of taking care of the tablets. The ancestral tablets reflect not only the importance of filial piety in Confucian thought but also reverence for the dead.

Oh my ancestors, please protect the family from harm. Keep us safe and sound.

The Origins of the Ancestral Tablet I

The Story of Jie Zitui

During the Warring States Period, Prince Chong'er of Jin fled from the enemies and went to live in exile.

When he was dying of hunger, one of his men, Jie Zitui, cut off a piece of meat from his leg, cooked it and offered it to Chong'er.

Later, Chong'er returned to his country and came into power. As Duke Wen, he rewarded those officials who had led a wandering life with him in those hard times.

Quick, bring Jie Zitui. I want to thank him properly.

He has taken his old mother to Mt Mianshan. He won't leave the place to accept a reward.

I'll have to go to him personally.

Jie Zitui still won't come out. What should I do?

Men! Start a fire. That should force him out.

Yes, Your Lordship!

The fire raged for three days and nights. Still, there was no sign of Jie Zitui.

Your Lordship, we've found Jie Zitui. But he's been burnt to death under a pine tree.

I killed him!

Cut down the pine and make a wooden tablet from it. I wish to pray to him.

Later, the custom of making tablets in memory of the dead spread.

The Origins of the Ancestral Tablet II
Ding Lan Carves Statues of His Parents

During the Eastern Han Dynasty, there was a man called Ding Lan. His parents passed away when he was young.

My parents died early and I didn't get a chance to repay them.

I can carve statues of my parents and worship them. I'll burn joss sticks for them day and night to show my filial piety.

My husband tells me to bow to these two figures every day. It's so annoying!

Prick you! Prick, prick!

The spots where they've been pricked are bleeding! Their eyes are wet with tears!

How dare you treat my parents in this way! Go back to your parents! You're no longer my wife.

The story of Ding Lan who made wooden statues of his parents spread. People started to copy him. Eventually, the statues evolved into tablets made to remember one's loved ones who had passed away.

SWEEPING THE TOMB

It drizzles and drizzles in this Pure Brightness Season,
I feel heavy at heart, a wayfarer on his way.
When I asked where a tavern might be found,
The cowherd points yonder to Apricot Flowering Village.

This is a famous Tang poem. The "Pure Brightness Season" mentioned in the poem is the season when the Chinese visit the cemetery to sweep the tombs of their deceased loved ones.

In olden days, five-coloured paper was placed on the grave with a stone put on top of it as a paperweight. It indicated that someone had visited the grave, and that it had not been abandoned.

Weeds on the tomb were pulled out and repair work was done where necessary. Then, the grave was covered with more earth and twigs of willow were stuck on it.

One should bow while burning hell money.

Usually, the family would bring some food and wine as offerings to the ancestors.

Sweeping the Tomb

THE NETHERWORLD

The Chinese have this saying: The good will be rewarded with good, and evil with evil. If reward or punishment is not forthcoming, it is because the time has not arrived.

Those who have done evil may escape punishment while still alive. But they can never escape punishment in Hell when they die. So don't ever carry things too far. Otherwise, when you've turned into a ghost, you'll suffer terribly.

King Yama literally means the "ruler of Hell". He metes out punishment and gives rewards in the netherworld. There are 10 Yama kings, each placed in charge of one court.

When a person dies, his good and bad deeds will be reflected in the *Register of Births and Deaths*.

The most wicked proceed to the Platform of Evil Mirror to see for themselves the sins they committed when they were alive.

After they have been judged by King Yama and the sentences have been meted out, they will be sent to different torture chambers for their punishments.

It is said that Hell has 18 levels, each of which has a different form of punishment. For example, malicious gossips have their tongues cut off. The most wicked ones are dumped into a cauldron to suffer the worst of pains and never see the light of day again.

After the punishment, they return to the Wheel of Rebirth. People who have done more good than evil in their past lives are born into good families. Evil ones are born as animals in their next lives.

In Chinese Buddhism, there is the doctrine of the Six-segment Wheel. The six segments are Heaven, Man, Asura, Animals, Hungry Ghosts and Hell.

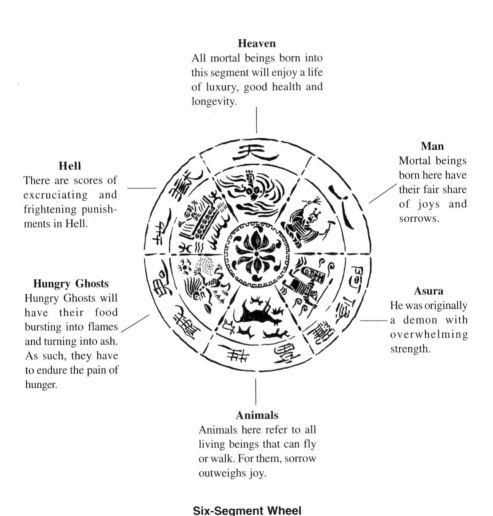

Heaven
All mortal beings born into this segment will enjoy a life of luxury, good health and longevity.

Man
Mortal beings born here have their fair share of joys and sorrows.

Hell
There are scores of excruciating and frightening punishments in Hell.

Hungry Ghosts
Hungry Ghosts will have their food bursting into flames and turning into ash. As such, they have to endure the pain of hunger.

Asura
He was originally a demon with overwhelming strength.

Animals
Animals here refer to all living beings that can fly or walk. For them, sorrow outweighs joy.

Six-Segment Wheel

Granny Meng's tea

Before all souls can be reincarnated, they must first have a serving of Granny Meng's tea. The tea has been spiked with a drug that will erase all of one's memories. This is to ensure that reborn souls will start their next life on a clean slate.

Black and White Guards of Impermanence

Hell has two infamous ghost guards — Black Guard of Impermanence and White Guard of Impermanence. It is said that when a person's time is up, King Yama will send these two guards to escort the person down to the netherworld.

The Black Guard of Impermanence has a fearsome countenance and inscribed on his headgear are the words "Death visits those who meet me". He is in charge of hunting down diabolical spirits. The White Guard of Impermanence has a kind and friendly air about him. Written on his headgear are the words "Fortune greets those who meet me". He guides the spirits of kind people to the netherworld. Later, people even revere him as the God of Fortune.

Oxhead Guard and Horseface Guard

This equally-famous duo comprises Oxhead Guard and Horseface Guard. It is said that they were an ox and a horse in their previous lives. To reward them for their hard work, King Yama appointed them as ghost guards.

The King of Ksitigarbha

The King of Ksitigarbha is one of the four great bodhisattvas in Buddhism. Though he could have attained enlightenment, he vowed to save all mortal beings before doing so. He was reputed to have declared: "As long as Hell is not empty, I will not attain enlightenment." He was said to be Maudgalyayana in a previous life.

Maudgalyayana and the Hungry Ghosts Festival

The Chinese believe that during the seventh month of the lunar calendar, the gates of Hell are thrown wide open and hordes of ghosts will pour into the mortal world. As such, people will hold ceremonies to expiate the sins of these wandering spirits. This period came to be known as the Hungry Ghosts Festival or the Yulan Basin Party.

This festival is believed to have originated from Maudgalyayana's attempt to save his mother. Apparently, his mother died and fell into Hell. There, she had to compete with hungry ghosts for food. Maudgalyayana had the power of clairvoyance and could see the plight his mother was in. He tried to send her food but when it reached his mother's hands, it would burst into flames and turn into ash.

In the end, the Buddha instructed him to make yearly offerings to spirits of the 10 quarters on the 15th day of the seventh month. His mother's ordeal thus came to an end. Therefore, the Hungry Ghosts Festival is a chance for children to repay their parents by releasing them from their suffering. It later took on a superstitious tone and its original significance gradually faded into oblivion.

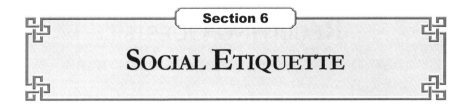

SOCIAL ETIQUETTE

The Chinese are a hospitable people. They have a host of social rules that govern everyday activities like meeting people and receiving gifts.

RECEIVING GUESTS

The Chinese place great importance on courtesy and socially accepted behaviour. Therefore, social etiquette has to be observed.

These rules serve to please both the host and the guest. If your guest is happy with the respect you show him, you'll feel proud too.

Li, have a cup of tea.

Great tea!

Offering tea

It is a custom to offer a cup of tea to your guest. Whether you belong to the upper class or are just an ordinary man, whether you are at a social function, at work, at home, on a trip or in any other situation, tea is served when you entertain a guest.

When the host offers tea, he should do so with both hands to show respect. The cup should be three-quarters full, not filled to the brim. The guest then accepts the tea with both hands and takes a few sips, whether he's thirsty or not. This is to show respect and appreciation.

Accepting gifts

When a guest comes for a visit, he will usually bring with him a gift. The host should thank him and accept it graciously. The guest will be embarrassed if his gift is not accepted. Never open the gift before the guest as this is considered extremely rude.

Seeing the guest off

When the guest leaves, ask him to stay a while longer. Or invite him to come back again. The host should stand up to see him to the door.

Upon seeing him out, watch him go until he is some distance away. Never turn your back as soon as you have said goodbye as this is rude.

If the guest is your senior or someone elderly, walk him downstairs, or even to the bus stop, or hail a cab for him.

MEETING PEOPLE

A bow with hands clasped

Clasp your hands to show acknowledgement. This is done in non-official functions when you're with people you know well.

A deeper bow with hands clasped

Clasp your hands, raise them high up then down. This is a show of great respect.

Bow

Keep your legs together and your hands at the side. Bend your body to show respect.

Handshake

Both parties stretch out their right hands. Remove your gloves if you're wearing them before shaking hands. If the other party is a lady, wait for her to stretch out her hand first. A light, short shake is good enough. Beyond that is regarded as rude.

Stepping up to the other party

When you see a friend or relative or someone older than you whom you have not met for a long time, take a few quick steps towards him. Shake his hands and greet him to show respect.

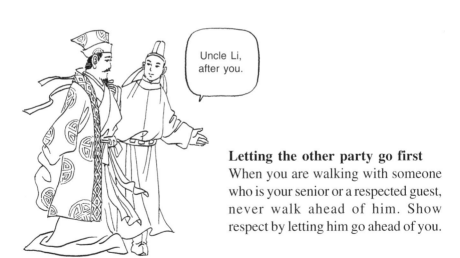

Letting the other party go first

When you are walking with someone who is your senior or a respected guest, never walk ahead of him. Show respect by letting him go ahead of you.

Ancient Social Etiquette

Kowtow
This was a show of deep respect for the monarch.

Bowing with knees on the ground
This was used between two persons of equal status. Later, it was used when one party had a big favour to ask of another party.

Good-fortune curtsy
This applied only to women in olden days. During the Tang Dynasty, women curtsied on meeting other people. This was done by placing both hands at the right waist, locking the hands and fingers together and bending the knees to show respect. As they bowed, they would wish the other party "may you have good fortune".

Wishing good health (woman)
Women put both their hands on their knees, which were both touching the ground, and bow.

Wishing good health (man)
This was to show respect for the elders. One knee touched the ground while the other leg was bent.

GIVING GIFTS

When attending a celebratory dinner, the gifts for the hosts are usually fruit, fabric, cash, artefacts or essential items used in a family.

If you receive a gift from a guest, the gift you give him in future must be of greater value than his. It is rude not to return his kindness.

Offer gifts in pairs. An even number symbolises good luck and a good ending.

In some places, it is taboo to use these articles as gifts:

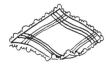

Handkerchief
It connotes parting with a person forever.

Scissors
Scissors connote the severing of ties.

Umbrella
To give an umbrella would mean a breakup.

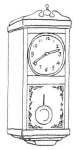

Don't give things in pairs to a sick person. No one wants misfortune to strike twice.

Flowers
Avoid giving jasmines or plum blossoms to businessmen. The former sounds exactly like *moli* 没利 (business losses) while the latter sounds like *mei* 霉 (bad luck).

Clock
It is taboo to give a clock as a birthday gift. "Giving a clock" (*songzhong* 送钟) sounds like "burying one's parent" (送终).

Red packets

In olden days, red was associated with life. As such, the Chinese revere the colour red. They use red paper to wrap things up as a sign of celebration and to ward off evil. Red packets are given away at weddings and birthdays, and also during Chinese New Year.

Red peas

Red peas are also popular as a love token among the Chinese. Red peas are also known as love peas.

Sending the Feather
of a Swan Over
Thousands of *Li*

It's a long and hazardous journey. I have to be very careful.

During the Tang Dynasty, an official who was stationed at the borders wanted to send a gift to the emperor.

Mian Bogao, this swan is a gift for the emperor. Take good care of it.

Yes, Sir!

One day...

Oh no! I'll be beheaded!

Your Majesty, my master offered a swan to you as a gift.

Unfortunately, the swan flew away due to my carelessness. It left behind just a feather.

Please punish me.

Ha ha... You travelled thousands of *li* to bring me this feather. Though the gift is nothing to shout about, your sincerity cannot be doubted. You're forgiven.

A Brief Chronology of Chinese History

	夏 Xia Dynasty		About 2100 – 1600 BC
	商 Shang Dynasty		About 1600 – 1100 BC
周 Zhou Dynasty	西周 Western Zhou Dynasty		About 1100 – 771 BC
	東周 Eastern Zhou Dynasty		770 – 256 BC
	春秋 Spring and Autumn Period		770 – 476 BC
	戰國 Warring States		475 – 221 BC
	秦 Qin Dynasty		221 – 207 BC
漢 Han Dynasty	西漢 Western Han		206 BC – AD 24
	東漢 Eastern Han		25 – 220
三國 Three Kingdoms	魏 Wei		220 – 265
	蜀漢 Shu Han		221 – 263
	吳 Wu		222 – 280
	西晉 Western Jin Dynasty		265 – 316
	東晉 Eastern Jin Dynasty		317 – 420
南北朝 Northern and Southern Dynasties	南朝 Southern Dynasties	宋 Song	420 – 479
		齊 Qi	479 – 502
		梁 Liang	502 – 557
		陳 Chen	557 – 589
	北朝 Northern Dynasties	北魏 Northern Wei	386 – 534
		東魏 Eastern Wei	534 – 550
		北齊 Northern Qi	550 – 577
		西魏 Western Wei	535 – 556
		北周 Northern Zhou	557 – 581
	隋 Sui Dynasty		581 – 618
	唐 Tang Dynasty		618 – 907
五代 Five Dynasties	後梁 Later Liang		907 – 923
	後唐 Later Tang		923 – 936
	後晉 Later Jin		936 – 946
	後漢 Later Han		947 – 950
	後周 Later Zhou		951 – 960
宋 Song Dynasty	北宋 Northern Song Dynasty		960 – 1127
	南宋 Southern Song Dynasty		1127 – 1279
	遼 Liao Dynasty		916 – 1125
	金 Jin Dynasty		1115 – 1234
	元 Yuan Dynasty		1271 – 1368
	明 Ming Dynasty		1368 – 1644
	清 Qing Dynasty		1644 – 1911
	中華民國 Republic of China		1912 – 1949
	中華人民共和國 People's Republic of China		1949 –

CHINESE CULTURE SERIES
150x210mm, fully illustrated, 160-192 pages

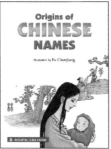

Chinese Imperial Women

The harem was a place where only the most beautiful, intelligent, fortunate and ruthless women could rise to the top. This book tells the stories of these women, the outstanding, the outrageous, the glorious and the tragic ones of the Chinese imperial harem.
160pp, ISBN 978-981-229-482-1

NEW

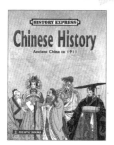

Chinese History: Ancient China to 1911

This book will help you to comprehend and interpret China's history in its proper context, plus provide vivid illustrations, and questions and answers to enhance your appreciation of great people and happenings.
192pp, ISBN 981-229-439-2

Great Chinese Emperors: Tales of Wise and Benevolent Rule

Read the tales of wise and benevolent rulers including Shennong, Li Shimin (Tang dynasty) and Emperor Kangxi (Qing dynasty). These stand tall for their outstanding contributions and character.
192pp, ISBN 981-229-451-1

Infamous Chinese Emperors: Tales of Tyranny and Misrule

Stories of China's most notorious emperors who are a motley crew of squanderers, murderers, thugs and lechers, and how they got their just deserts!
192pp, ISBN 981-229-459-7

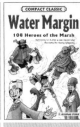

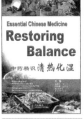

中华习俗的故事

编著　：李小香
绘画　：傅春江
翻译　：吴杰欣

亚太图书有限公司出版